Food Truck Business

Discover How to Plan, Run and Manage a Successful Food Business

(Easy Way From Business Plan and Startup to Profits and Scaling)

Logan Duffey

Published By **Phil Dawson**

Logan Duffey

All Rights Reserved

Food Truck Business: Discover How to Plan, Run and Manage a Successful Food Business (Easy Way From Business Plan and Startup to Profits and Scaling)

ISBN 978-1-77485-993-3

No part of this guidebook shall be reproduced in any form without permission in writing from the publisher except in the case of brief quotations embodied in critical articles or reviews.

Legal & Disclaimer

The information contained in this ebook is not designed to replace or take the place of any form of medicine or professional medical advice. The information in this ebook has been provided for educational & entertainment purposes only.

The information contained in this book has been compiled from sources deemed reliable, and it is accurate to the best of the Author's knowledge; however, the Author cannot guarantee its accuracy and validity and cannot be held liable for any errors or omissions. Changes are periodically made to this book. You must consult your doctor or get professional medical advice before using any of the suggested remedies, techniques, or information in this book.

Upon using the information contained in this book, you agree to hold harmless the Author from and against any damages, costs, and expenses, including any legal fees potentially resulting from the application of any of the information provided by this guide. This disclaimer applies to any damages or injury caused by the use and application, whether directly or indirectly, of any advice or information presented, whether for breach of contract, tort, negligence, personal injury, criminal intent, or under any other cause of action.

You agree to accept all risks of using the information presented inside this book. You need to consult a professional medical practitioner in order to ensure you are both able and healthy enough to participate in this program.

Table Of Contents

Chapter 1: Why Marketing Is Important .. 1

Chapter 2: Food Truck Vehicle Wraps 6

Chapter 3: How To Get A Website Dome For $0.99... 15

Chapter 4: Don't Pay For A Expensive Web Designer... 22

Chapter 5: Using Press Releases To Your Advantage... 31

Chapter 6: Getting More Facebook Likes 41

Chapter 7: Food Truck Marketing On Youtube 53

Chapter 8: Getting Your Food Truck Business Listed On Yelp........................... 68

Chapter 9: Customer Reward Programmes 81

Chapter 1: Why Marketing Is Important

This book is about food trucks marketing. I think everyone understands marketing. I've come across many people that started food truck companies and have had the opportunity to learn from a variety of experiences. Some have never even heard of business, while others have been in business for years. A brief introduction is needed to ensure I don't leave anyone behind. Most people know what marketing is and how it works. Some people, especially those who are new to the business, may be confused about marketing.

Before I get into this subject, and leave some people in wonder, let me first explain what marketing is. Marketing is, in many ways, a very simple concept. However, it can often be made too complicated. Marketing, in a nutshell is any activity that puts your company and products in front a potential customer. Marketing activities could include advertising, sales and pricing strategies, product packaging or customer service. All of these activities are typically planned and tested with a goal to grow a business, build a reputation and ultimately increase revenues.

A customer-centric approach to marketing is essential.

* The Needs

* What you want

* Requirements

Marketing is challenging because what customers want, need or desire is constantly changing. Marketers must be able and willing to adjust to that change. It's possible for what is working right now to not be effective in the future.

Market success also depends on how you get your message across and to the right target audience. Your marketing efforts should be targeted at vegan food trucks, and not just burger lovers. Your customer's needs are the basis of your marketing. You can't make a great product sell if you don't get it in front people who want it, need it and will pay you for it.

In terms of marketing, many business owners fall short of their customers' expectations. Even if your product or service is the best, if it doesn't meet the needs and desires of your customers, you won't be able to sell it.

Marketing begins with getting to know your customer and what they want. Even though you have a great idea for your food truck, you must talk to customers to test it out. These early testing can help you decide if your concept, theme or menu is viable, as well as the attitude and quality of your customers.

Marketing is not a one-size fits all approach. No amount of PR and advertising will fix it. There are many methods to market a company or service. Although most businesses share the same marketing tactics, some have unique marketing plans. I believe food truck business owners can utilize unique marketing tactics that are relevant to the industry.

Marketing can take on many different forms in today's business environment. There are many tools that can be used and many channels available to market businesses. Marketing can take the form of a simple flyer printed on paper that is copied and passed to people. Or it can be more complicated with complex planning and productions. Marketing has no set rules. A successful marketing plan requires creativity and research.

Some people are very imaginative in how they communicate their messages to customers and prospects. Some people just have the natural ability to generate ideas that promote businesses. Marketing is not something that everyone can do well. Ideas can be shared with your partner or other staff members. You might be surprised at what you find. You might already be a marketing genius! In certain cases, you may need to hire marketing specialists to create a profitable marketing plan. While this may add some extra cost to your food truck operation, the benefits can outweigh the additional expense.

While there are many aspects to marketing a food-truck business, they all come together to help you grow your business. Some strategies are long-term and others are quick promotions around holidays and special events. While a lot of it will be accessible online through social media, some of the information is tangible on a daily basis.

The next chapter will address the most visible component of your marketing efforts. This includes your vehicle and its appearance. While this is all about appearances it can be a great way to make customers notice your car! As if you judge a book's cover by its cover.

Chapter 2: Food Truck Vehicle Wraps

The wrap on your food truck's outside is the most important piece of physical branding. It instantly tells potential buyers who you are as well as what type of business it is. This is your brand identity. It should be bright and colorful. Your logo should be easily visible from a distance. Your truck graphics need to be unique and catch the attention of others. You can make the difference between an excellent truck wrap and a fantastic one by choosing the right graphic artist.

While many of the marketing strategies described in this book can be done at a very reasonable cost, truck wraps will seem expensive when compared with other marketing costs discussed in this guide. Your food truck's wrap cost can vary from $1500 to more than $6000. This is a rough estimate. To receive an accurate price, you would need to give the vehicle wrap company your make and model. The vehicle wrap company can use pre-existing templates to figure out the amount of vinyl needed and how each piece attaches to the exterior. A new template may be required if the vehicle you're using is not compatible with an existing template.

You can advertise your food truck wrap by using a variety of effective methods. This could vary depending on where it is located. Even if your food truck isn't open for business, you can still advertise your company up to 24 hours per day by placing it in front of the public. If your food truck wrap is visible enough, people will associate your delicious food with it. This can help to build brand recognition and awareness.

Wraps for food trucks are usually applied within 1 to 3 working days depending on the size and area of the surface. There may be delays if there are intricate parts on your vehicle. Once the process is started, your installer can provide you with accurate times. Vinyl wrap on your truck can last five years or longer depending on how you take care of it. You should avoid high-pressure power washing your truck and use anything that will damage the vinyl. The length of the warranty the installer gives you for your wrap is an important thing to consider as a business owner. You should find out what the installer will do for your business if the wrap becomes peeling or detached quickly. Most wraps for vehicles will last longer than your food truck's lifetime.

Can I make any changes to a wrap?

Vehicle wraps have a lot more versatility than painting. I get that things can change in business. But what if your phone number changes, or your Twitter handle changes? Maybe your logo needs to be changed. This type of information can be easily modified on your truck - even with a wrap!

The wrap company has the ability to edit the computer and only print the vinyl overlays needed for your specific area. The process is very smooth and you don't have pay extra to have the truck re-wrapped. It is possible to only see edges of the newly applied sections.

But even that is nearly impossible to spot unless your eyes are open.

You can make minor changes to any section of your wrap by simply applying a sticker to your truck. The contract installers will align the new graphics so they look just like the original wrap. This method can be used to repair damaged sections of your wrap. The wrap installers can cut out the damaged section, reprint that area, and apply the vinyl again. Your wrap should look like new.

Wraps that Save You Money

Your vehicle wrap should provide the best value. Wrapping a food truck can be costly. A step van can take a lot to cover. The time it takes to apply the vinyl is another factor. How would you like to save money on your food trucks graphics, while still maintaining a beautiful truck? How could that impact your marketing budget

It might not be obvious, but not all food trucks need to be wrapped. Some food truck owners have limited budgets and only use die-cut logos. This allows for less vinyl, lower application costs, and less time to design. Many food truck owners are very happy with the results of simply applying a logo decal over the base of their truck. Look out for trucks that have a full wrap instead of decals next time you're out. Surprised at the number that don't have full wraps? I have seen a lot of trucks with gorgeous full-color wraps, and they always grab my attention!

Even if you add minor graphics or a logo to your truck's exterior, be sure the vehicle's underneath surface is clean and attractive. I don't mean to leave visible scratches or rust on your truck's exterior. You want your graphics applied on smooth surfaces that will enhance your logo. It is very important to position it. If you leave the side panels open, will it still be visible? If not will it be visible if you open the side panels?

It is possible to have your phone numbers, website addresses, and other details printed on vinyl that is adhered onto the exterior panels of your truck. These small pieces of vinyl can include your business information. It is possible to reduce the time required to apply graphics to your truck, even if you don't have to do a full wrap. If you are able, use your truck's current exterior color. While most trucks will be white or grey, you can still use the existing color to give your graphics a standout look.

You could paint the truck in one color and then put vinyl graphics on the outside. You will pay more if your food truck is painted.

The Production Process

Wrap companies are committed to helping you create the perfect wrap design. You can often work with them one-on-1 to get the look that you want. During the design phase, it is important that you can see how your design comes together. During the design phase you should request previews and any changes. This will save you time and help you communicate your concerns. Your designer will appreciate it!

Once the designs are complete, your designer should email you mock-ups, explanations, as well as the final proof, before the design goes to printing. Before the design is sent to printer, you must approve or suggest any changes. It is best to make any modifications while the design still exists in the computer. Otherwise, you may incur higher expenses.

Many wrap companies have their own large-format printers once your graphics are ready for print. Check out previous wraps to see if they are similar to yours. You can check the wrap's finish and see if they have any other options before you make them print. If everything is in order, give them permission to begin the printing process.

Wrap companies often have their very own facilities in which they wrap vehicles. They will usually have a warehouse or large garage to fit vehicles of all sizes. They may also rent or share warehouses with other companies to reduce overhead.

Remember that you may need to travel to apply your wrap to your truck. Sometimes, you may live in an area that does not have a wrap contractor. If this is the case, your food truck will need to be brought to them so they can work on your vehicle. It could be hundreds of kilometers away, or even farther! Keep in mind, however, that you don't necessarily have to be located in the same town as the wrap business for the design phase. All of this can be done over the telephone or online.

The wrap company will also wrap windows on your truck if they have them. Keep in mind, however, that vinyl will not be applied to the front windshield and the windows on the sides. They may be able to use perforated Vinyl to wrap the windows. This is especially important when wrapping rear windows. While the design may look seamless from the outside, it will not appear seamless inside.

However, you can still see out from the inside but it will be impaired slightly. Imagine this happening on a city bus. You've seen the buses that are wrapped in a moving billboard. Everything, including windows, is covered up on the bus.

Surprisingly, the exterior bus looks almost seamless. However, passengers can still see the windows through the many dots punched into vinyl sections. It's similar to looking through a flyscreen except that it is denser.

Chapter 3: How To Get A Website Dome For $0.99

If you don't have an online presence for your business in today's digital world, you are likely to lose a lot of potential customers. It's shocking to see how many small business owners don't own websites or have only minimal information. Many smaller sites don't look professional. Your website will be the first contact a customer makes with you. They want to know more about you and your trucks, and they also want to explore your menus and prices.

It's easy and inexpensive to create a quality website. Websites don't have to cost a lot to look as good as the ones your competition offers. There is a common misconception that a great web designer and hosting plan will cost thousands of dollars. I can assure you, it is possible with a minimal budget while still maintaining a professional look. You don't even need programming knowledge or technical expertise to make it happen. This can save you lots of money. But where do I start?

It is essential that you have a domain name. Although it should not be difficult to create a domain name, it will require careful consideration. The domain name will be your website address. For example, if your truck is called Crispy Grilled Cheese then you ideally would want to get CrispyGrilledCheese.com as your address. Domain names can be found on sale for a low price. While most domain registrars charge between $10 and $15 per year to register a.com domain, this tip will show you how you can save $0.99 on your first year.

How to Get 99 Cents Domain Name

Here's how I can get domains for as low as 0.99 cents. This requires GoDaddy to act as your webhost and domain registrar. I'll be talking more about hosting later. This will save you some money, but it is a good idea for your business. My preferred domain extension would be.com. This trick can only be used for.com domains. Let's see what you can do... it's totally legal.

* Google the term "Godaddy" and leave out the quotation marks

GoDaddy almost always has a sponsored Listing for 0.99 domains, at the top end of search results

* Click on this GoDaddy link

* GoDaddy's main website allows you to search for domain names by entering the desired information.

* If you have a domain name that is not already taken, add it to your cart

* If your domain is not available, please choose another name

* Check out to receive the discount

Please note that this $0.99 price does not apply to subsequent years and is only available for domain names ending in.com. I buy many domain names each year. For the most part, I never pay more than 0.99 each. Please note that I am not associated to GoDaddy. They do host my websites and I save money by using this trick.

Hosting Website

Hosting is the second component of your website. Without a hosting account, you can't have your website. It's where your website's files can be stored. Visitors can access them whenever they visit your site. It functions in the same way as an external hard-drive. Your content, graphics, code and other data are all stored on the host. There are many web hosting companies, but this is the type that I recommend for self-hosting. Self-hosting gives you the most freedom because you can customize everything (if that's what you know).

You should also check out these hosting companies:

* GoDaddy

* BlueHost

* HostGator

* Dreamhost

It's simple to sign up both for domain hosting and webhosting. As a new customer, it's even easier as you can buy both the domain and the webhosting simultaneously. The servers automatically link your domain to the main folder. New customers may get discounts on hosting.

This is very simple work that you can do all by yourself. Paying a web design company or another company to do this will cost you money for services that you can do on your computer. This may seem complicated, but it is easy to do. The steps are clearly described on the hosting company's website during the signup process.

Do I need a separate hosting account for every website I have?

If you've never owned your own website, you would usually buy the domain along with hosting. These two elements are the building blocks of any website. If you already have your website and have a hosting plan, you do not need another account to launch a second website. Another domain name will suffice. You will only need one hosting account if you have multiple websites. Your hosting account works like a hard drive. Every website's content can be found in different folders on your server. Each domain accesses the data in its own folder.

Consider this: If you already have your own website and want to set up a website about your food truck business, you can still use the same host for your tee business. If you want to create a new website or start a business, you can use the same host. The new website will need a brand new domain. I have a method to get domains for as low as .99 cents.

In some instances, you might need another host to host your second website. I made the mistake once of buying a basic account that only allowed one site to be stored. I think I was just trying to save money, not knowing what I was doing. While I would have preferred to only need one website, it became apparent that I needed multiple sites.

Avoid making the same mistake that I did. Make sure you check the terms and conditions of the hosting account that you sign up for. In my example I selected Economy hosting over Deluxe hosting at GoDaddy. But most hosts allow you multiple websites using the same hosting account. This is all to ensure that you have the best possible options so that you do not face any problems later on, should you wish to add websites.

While this information is not directly related to marketing, I think it's important to know, especially if the website will be for your food truck.

Chapter 4: Don't Pay For A Expensive Web Designer

Okay, I explained to you that you can do basic hosting and domain configuration on your computer. You might be surprised to know that you can also set up your website yourself. That's right! It doesn't take a web developer to make a website you love. Save a lot of time and money by building your own website. It is easy to do and you don't even need to know programming.

I still don't know HTML and coding. Even though I don't understand CSS, I still hear these terms in relation to website creation. Yet, I can create multiple websites very easily. Is that possible, you might ask? WordPress is a fantastic platform. You may have heard of this platform.

WordPress is not only for bloggers

WordPress was originally created for bloggers. It's not only for bloggers. WordPress can power both small and larger businesses.

Here are some real food truck owners who use WordPress to power WordPress websites.

Seoulful Philly - http://www.seoulfullphilly.com

Purple People Eatery - http://www.purpleppleatery.com

JapaCurry. http://japacurry.com

Liba Falafel - http://libafalafel.com

Barbed Wire Reef - http://www.barbedwirereef.com

Wheels on Fire - http://wheelsonfirepizza.com

Ladybird Food Truck - http://ladybirdfoodtruck.com

I hope you can visit them all. While it is possible for those food trucks to have web designers create the sites, they are still very easy to make. Each one started as templates. Once you learn how each works, you will be able to use almost any WordPress theme. This is how I see it: If you can fill out web forms and create online Christmas cards, you should be able use WordPress.

WordPress is free to download and use, including templates. You can get a website for free if WordPress is new to you.

http://wordpress.com

This is where you will be able to set up a WordPress site free of charge. You can then see firsthand how it works, before going for the self-hosted option which involves purchasing a domain host service. However, there is one downside to building a WordPress.com web site. Your web address won't be as simple as your name for a food truck. Consider, for instance, that your truck is called Heavy Burger. Your website URL would look like this:

Is that the ".wordpress" text at the URL's end? This is the result using WordPress free for your website. While this is completely usable, it can be hard for customers to remember. It also doesn't look very professional. Many food trucks and businesses use this website. However, you will probably see that it is not ideal.

WordPress offers additional services such a custom domain. One solution is to charge WordPress. This option could be available if you already have a website built on WordPress.com and don't feel like rebuilding it from scratch on your own hosting service. If you pay for premium WordPress.com services, you can have a custom domain name (get rid.wordpress.com), additional data storage, or remove ads from the site.

Start by creating a test site

To get a feel for the interface, it is a good idea first to create a Wordpress.com Test website. It's simple and you only need an email address to set it up. You can use an alternate email address for the test account than your main email.

You should become familiar with the buttons and tabs. It shouldn't take too long to grasp the basics. Click and test things. It is a testing website.

These are just a few of the things that you should do once you've signed up.

* Create a blog posting

* Upload an image to a blog post

* Insert a YouTube clip into your blog

* Upload your logo

* Search for WordPress themes

* Modify your WordPress theme

* Add a blog entry

* Schedule a blog posting

* Connect your Facebook, Twitter, or Instagram feeds to your site

* Share your test post on Facebook and Twitter

These are the most important things to know about running a WordPress site. You'll be able run your site confidently if all the items are done correctly. It's very easy to use WordPress, even for non-technical people.

Advanced WordPress Techniques

WordPress is capable of so much more. However, I decided to simplify the process and help you set up a test site to get you started. To help you get to grips with the advanced features of WordPress, I'll touch on them.

WordPress has a strong SEO and search engine optimization. WordPress can help your website appear in search engines like Google Bing Yahoo and Bing. You need to provide relevant parameters about your website that match what people are searching. This is not an SEO tutorial. However, a few keystrokes can increase the chances that your website will be found in a Google search.

Title Descriptions and Tags

Only a title is required for each post. That's it. The most important thing is to make sure that the title of your post clearly and concisely explains what it is about. Attention must also be paid to the optional sections of your posting. These include the description, tags, and other optional parts.

After you are done with your post, make sure to fill in the fields for the description or tags. The description is clear and concise, but it has a limit on the characters that will appear in a search results. The maximum length is usually 160 characters. When you write your description, try to sum up your post in 2 sentences. It's possible to be longer, but search engines won't read any more than 160 characters.

Tags can be described as keywords that are relevant and useful for your post. Once you are done writing your description, add tags or keywords to your blog post. These words can be as simple as single words and will help search engines to determine the topic of your post. While you don't have time to think about these things, it is important to be able to identify keywords from your blog posts.

SEO Tips

Food trucks can be unique businesses. They are usually located in a single area or market. This is important to remember as you add tags and write your description. If you want people to find your business, they should search for the type of food that you serve and the location where you are located.

Let's suppose, for example, that you have a food cart in Phoenix called Big Daddy barbecue. There are several popular BBQ items on your menu. If you're looking for restaurants, people may be searching for a specific type of BBQ. These are some keywords to use when searching for this food truck company:

* Big Daddy BBQ

* BBQ pulled-pork restaurant

* Authentic BBQ Phoenix

* Phoenix BBQ restaurant

* Phoenix food truck

Scottsdale BBQ

* Best BBQ In Phoenix

* Southern barbecue

* Phoenix BBQ Catering

I think you get it. Local emphasis is important as your main customers are local. Some keywords do not need to include your city's name but some should. This is also true for your description. It is important to include your city name in the description, as it will make it more relevant to searches.

This is a very basic explanation of SEO. If you can apply some of this knowledge on your website you will be miles ahead other food trucks that do not pay attention to this stuff. Although it requires a little more work, the overall process is not that difficult.

Chapter 5: Using Press Releases To Your Advantage

The ideal tool for getting a company's message to the media has been press releases. It's a tool that has a lot of nostalgia and is still used by large companies. What about food truck and other small businesses? Are press releases effective even when you're not an enormous corporation? Let's explore!

It is human nature to want information and current news. There are many news outlets, even within your local area. Press releases can be powerful tools for building your brand and credibility when they are done properly. Press releases are a great tool to promote your products and services. It's your food truck and what they have to offer. This is not traditional advertising. However, it can create trust and build your brand through journalistic-like settings. It can look more trustworthy as the information you want is often made public in a newsworthy format.

Of course, many people have questions about when the press release should be sent. What is most newsworthy and important? Why didn't our press release get much attention? This chapter will teach you how to write press releases better and provide suggestions for what to do with your future PR efforts.

How to define your goals

The type of business that you run will dictate the content, timing, distribution and format of your press release. Because we're talking about food truck companies, it helps us reduce and eliminate ineffective methods. But, ultimately, you must ask yourself: What do you want your PR efforts for? Do you want:

* News/Media coverage

* Available for local and national coverage

* Product announcement

* Promotion announcement

* Event announcement

* Promoting charitable donations

* Foodie coverage

* Restaurant reviews

* New menu item

* Industry news

* Etc.

If you're approaching news outlets such television stations or newspapers, the most important question you need to answer is "Is it newsworthy?" It is not enough to give your addresses in a press release. News organizations need information that will appeal to a wide audience. If they are local newspapers or TV stations, they tend to focus heavily on local stories that affect the community.

What's so newsworthy about a food trailer? Consider these things:

* Partnering with non-profit organizations during times of need

* The largest icecream sundae

* We offer the most unique catering services

* Launching the most unusual truck

* Offering your assistance in times of crisis

These are just a few suggestions to help get you thinking about what is important about your business. While it would be fair for local media to give coverage, it can still be done depending on what your business offers.

Best time to target press releases

The news about your food trucks business is not likely to be considered newsworthy. However, news about your food truck business is not always about politics or crime. Focusing on reporters who report on human interest stories, and particularly lifestyle or food reporters, will yield the best results. You should be careful not to spam these reporters with press releases. It could lead to you being added to their SPAM mailing list.

It is best to notify reporters at least one week in advance of any newsworthy events so they can consider your story as well as the many other stories that they are handling. However, it is a good idea to send it out as soon as you can so that they have time to consider your event.

If you wish to voice your opinion about a current news story, reach out to reporters who have reported on the topic in the past. You can still provide your expert opinion on the story if it is still popular. One example is that there may be new zoning regulations in your city that could affect the way you do things. Your opinion could be offered and you could explain why or not the laws are favorable for your business. You might be passionate about a local charity. Your brand might be able to advertise your support by donating your services during an event.

Press releases can be powerful tools, but they must be used carefully and sparingly. For every thing you do, don't send out a press statement. Keep it to major events that will have a positive effect on people and your city. It is possible to make a positive impact with a good PR message and free publicity.

Press Releases - Wrong

Sending out your press release can lead to a flood in calls about your business. But what happens if the response is not positive? It is crucial to understand who your press releases are going to and how to address them to increase your chances for being picked up. Press releases should inspire excitement and intrigue. It needs to be interesting! Press releases should be concise and not ramble. It should be concise and straight to the point. Reporters have busy lives and will need to digest your information quickly. If they require additional information, they will contact you. Reporters recommend that you describe your story in the same way as a 6 year-old to maintain a simple narrative. Don't use technical terms. These can come later.

Reporters are always looking for stories to enhance their stories. So if you can get involved with an event that is newsworthy, you may have a better chance of getting attention from the reporter. Do your research on the reporter/organization you are targeting. Showing that you understand their business and what interests them, you will be more likely get the attention you need to write your story. Watch their videos, read some of the articles and get a feel about their style before contacting them.

Format for Press Release

If this is your first time writing a press release, you will need to be aware of the guidelines. There are seven major parts to a press statement. These parts don't have necessarily to be included, but more substance is better. Here's a list containing the most important parts of a Press Release:

* Headline

* Introduction

* Source

* Essentials

* Quotes

* Additional Information

* Contact Information

Each section is fairly self-explanatory. But this is the format most news agencies and reporters are familiar with. Your headline should be catchy and memorable right away. A dull headline won't get anyone's attention. You can show off your creativity here!

Here's a good example. Sushi Dog Dojo, a food truck, has created a new sushi roll hotdog that everyone should try. This headline could be very simple or it could show a lot of excitement. Let's take an overview:

Boring headline

Sushi Dog Dojo launches the Sushi Roll Hot Dog

Exciting Headline

Sushi Dog Dojo's Sushi roll hot dog is an amazing creation that amazes top Japanese chefs - A must try!

Can you notice the difference between this and the second example? You want your reporter to be interested in more of your story. Once you grab their attention, and they are interested in what you have to offer, they will read more.

Additional Suggestions

It is important to have good relationships when it comes down to business. Knowing who you are is just as important than what you know. It is always a good idea, before you contact them about anything, to make connections with members of the media. If you engage them before you have anything to pitch, you will both feel more relaxed and build a trusting relationship for the times when you need their assistance. It may be because of previous interactions.

You don't have to be annoying or pushy by pitching reporters. Instead, you can build a rapport with them so that you are both on friendly terms. These are some options to make contact.

* Connect with them using Social Media (Facebook and Twitter, LinkedIn, etc.

* If you're present at events, introduce your self to reporters

* Invite reporters for a tasting of your food

* Please leave comments for articles written and submitted by the reporter

* Be a regular blogger on a reporter's blog

* Attend meetings of the city council

* Approach reporters from smaller publications

* Join community events sponsored in part by the media

When a reporter contacts you for an interview, you must do everything you can to make it happen. Even if they ask that you complete it within 24 hours. Your flexibility and willingness to work with tight deadlines will impress. You might lose your job and be replaced by a competitor.

Stay in touch with reporters and editors if they contact you. Invite them to lunch at the truck, or even meet for coffee. It will help you remember who and what you are. You might consider hosting a tasting party with local media if you have a food truck business. A sampling event is also a good idea, especially if the food is free.

There are many different ways to make a PR plan work and I've just listed a few. Follow these steps to increase your chances of success in getting free publicity for food trucks.

Chapter 6: Getting More Facebook Likes

Facebook can be a powerful marketing tool that can help your business get more customers. However, you need to know how to use it properly. Facebook can provide incredible reach for the right audience. The statistics about Facebook users are amazing and continue to amaze researchers. Facebook boasts 1.3billion users and 680 million connect via mobile devices. Users between the ages of 18 and 34 are active on Facebook with 48% of them checking it as soon as they wake up, spending an average of 18 minutes per day! It is clear that you must create a Facebook Page for your food truck if you don't already have one.

Food Truck not yet operational

Even if the truck is not yet launched, you must still get one now and post on it. It is easier to plan what you will post on your page if the truck is running, but it can be hard to know what to do if the truck is still being built. This is the ideal time to keep people informed about your progress and get them excited about your next truck. Let's get personal about how you build your truck. It's important to show excitement when something is completed or you reach an important milestone.

You can build anticipation and connect with your audience by sharing behind-the-scenes information and images.

How to Get more Engagement

Increase your engagement with your followers by posting content more often. Your posting frequency will vary depending on your schedule, but I suggest posting 5 to 7 times per week to show your fans that you are still active on your Facebook page. Your Facebook page will have more engaged fans if you are perceived as being active by engaging with your followers.

You can share pictures and videos from your business's most exciting day to Facebook update. These are much better than posts that only contain text. People love to glance at their timeline and posts that include images or videos often attract more attention. The more people like you, the more Likes and comments you could get.

A picture post at the start can get you 1 like. This can happen to many of your image posts. Sometimes you won't get likes for your photo and may get frustrated. This is often a deterrent for many who try to build a Facebook fan base. However, if you can forget about those feelings and keep posting regularly, eventually you'll find the post that starts the momentum.

However, the quality of your content with your audience will determine how popular you are. Knowing what your customers want from your business is key. Experts have found that people prefer quick and easy posts because they are more likely to scan headlines and get the information they need. You don't just have to make your posts short, but you also need to appeal to them by educating, entertaining, or even informing them. These are just three of the many things

I will discuss in relation to food truck marketing.

Educational Posts - This type should help your followers learn something, just like the title suggests. Perhaps it's your best technique for cooking French fries or the best way marinate meat for the greatest flavor. Other people want to learn your skills.

I recall being asked by someone how to use ginger. She shared that she once made an awful dish because of ginger. I asked her how the ginger was incorporated into her dish. She said that she just chopped the ginger and mixed it into her dish. I reminded her that ginger can be strong and pungent so you only need to extract the essence. I instructed her to crush the ginger one-time with a knife before adding it to the dish. The ginger flavor will be infused in the rest of your ingredients, so you won't end eating the actual ginger. This advice was invaluable to my friend.

I get it that your business uses some proprietary methods and ingredients that you don't want others to know. Although you don't have to share your recipes, little bits of helpful information can help a lot. Good advice can help you be seen as an authority figure, someone who has the time and resources to help your followers.

Entertaining Posts-These posts can be about just about anything. However, it must be able attract and hold the reader's attention. These can be fun or quirky posts. If you're extremely busy you can post a short video of your chaotic kitchen when there is no end to the customers outside.

A couple of GoPro cameras can be mounted inside and outside your truck in order to capture any exciting events. The footage will need to edited before posting, but it's a good option to have a camera nearby without it getting in your way.

Enlightening Blogs - An article that combines all elements of the two previous categories can be called an enlightening one. You could show how your ingredients are sourced or how your profits go to charity as an example of an enlightening article. Here you can find information that is not commonly known about your company.

Some of these ideas are possible in food truck advertising.

Food images

Ingredient images

Images from food trucks

The team at work.

Your place or venue

Photos of special guests

Attendance at special events

Pictures of your truck at special landmarks

Close-ups from your truck's interior

Cooking tools

Daily menu specials

Signature dishes

Behind-the scenes photos

Impromptu photos during a service

Pictures of new products, menu items

Ingredient shopping trips

Problems mechanical

How to find time to post on Facebook

If you're trying your best to balance the seemingly endless to-do lists of your day, posting to Facebook daily can seem daunting. This is where your phone can come in handy. You can take your smartphone or tablet out whenever you're working on your food trucks and snap a picture of something you like or record a short video.

Even your employees can participate. Consider including them in your marketing plans. Your staff can also use their smartphones to take photos and videos suitable for posting on Facebook. Some business owners don't want employees to have full access to their company's Facebook account. That is perfectly understandable. An easy solution is to ask the owner to send you their media on your phone so that you can handle it yourself.

It is difficult to find time to post a blog post when you are busy. I will be introducing you to a technique known as 'batching,' which is used by many entrepreneurs to make their business more productive.

What is Batch posting?

Batching lets you combine tasks in one place, instead of trying to accomplish them over several days. Batching can also help you be more focused on the task in hand, which will allow you to do a better job. You can get in the zone faster and save time by batching.

Checking and responding to email messages is a great example of batching. Inboxes are constantly being fed with emails. Responding to each email is not a good use of your time.

It is possible to automate the email process for busy people by batching it. This means that you won't read or respond to email at the same time. Instead, find a time within the day that you can dedicate to only email-related tasks. Take a look through all your emails, and then respond to the senders who need your attention. If you receive many emails, it might be a good idea to set up a time for you to review them during the day, and again at night.

This is just one example, but batching can be applied to many related tasks. Batching is also used in food trucks to prepare food and shop for ingredients.

What Does Batching Mean for Facebook?

You might be wondering what the best way to batch Facebook posts? Facebook offers the ability to schedule posts. This is an important benefit for food trucks owners. It's no longer necessary to take a break from a busy job to post something to Facebook.

You can now schedule Facebook posts in advance and prepare for them. This means that you can create posts up to a week in advance and have them available to go live immediately when you want your followers.

Now you can strategically set posts that go live just as you open for business. Click the down button next to the publish button to access the scheduler. A dropdown menu appears. You can choose Schedule Post to select the publication date and time. After you have written your post, add any photos or videos to it, click on Schedule. You can continue this process until there are enough posts to go into the queue. This is it! Your posts are now live at the times and dates you specified.

Posts that can be repeated

We know how Facebook batches posts. I now want to discuss posts that should be scheduled on a regular basis. Now you have a schedule for your food truck. Most likely, you visit the same locations weekly. The Facebook scheduler can help you let your friends know where you will be on a particular day.

A batching session should include information about the places you'll be parking for the next week. These location posts could even be scheduled for a month. Most food truck owners have a good idea of where they will park in the coming month. It's best to schedule your posts at least half an hour before arriving at your location. This will allow your followers plenty of time to see the announcement and get to you. You've now automated one of the most important tasks in your marketing campaign!

Chapter 7: Food Truck Marketing On Youtube

Online video is an integral part of how we gather information and are entertained. YouTube is one the most well-known and popular video sharing websites. Each day, 300 minutes worth of video is uploaded to YouTube. YouTube makes sharing video easy by hosting user videos at no cost.

YouTube is an excellent tool for business promotion. When used properly, it can also help you build trust and brand recognition. YouTube is a sophisticated and complex social network. It may not look like it initially, but it's really quite the advanced social network. YouTube's interface is simple enough that uploaded videos can easily be shared on social media sites like Facebook, Twitter and blogs. YouTube videos can spread quickly, if they become famous or go viral. YouTube is an excellent tool to market food trucks.

Food truck owners are careful about how much they spend on their business. How can you leverage YouTube to boost and strengthen your marketing plans? These tips can help.

How to Shoot Your Videos

YouTube videos don't necessarily have to look fancy. Sometimes you can just have a few clips, while other times they can include multiple shots. While videos that contain more than one shot require editing, they can be much more interesting. You can add music to make it a finished video.

What Camera is Best?

There are many cameras to choose from when shooting marketing videos for your food trucks. While technology has changed over the years, I think it is much easier now to capture high quality video. Although you can still get a traditional video camera with internal memory cards and hard drives, many people are switching to digital video cameras.

Both point-and shoot and DSLR digital cameras are very popular and I use them to shoot my video. They're easy to use, and I love that you can shoot amazing photos as well as video with one camera. DSLRs are wonderful in that they have a cinematic feel but are more difficult to use. If I move around a lot, it can be difficult for a DSLR to maintain focus. I like the video I get when I have more time.

The camera is too small for DSLRs. Because of the camera's size, I don't find it necessary to carry my DSLR around much. It's difficult for me not to have this camera. I'm not the only person who feels this way. Many people I spoke to told me that they don't like taking their DSLR along because it adds bulk.

A small, point and shoot digital camera is my preference for video capturing. The compact size of the camera allows me to easily carry it around with me, without having to carry around a large camera bag. The quality of digital cameras is excellent and they can record video at 720p or 1080p HD. The point-

and shoot camera makes it easy to grab the camera and immediately start shooting.

One option I explored was using my mobile phone to record videos. This could include any smartphone. I don't use my iPhone for video, even though it has a lot of space on its internal hard drive. If you are an iPhone owner, you already know what I mean.

Low Cost Mobile Devices

I have shot a lot of video on my mobile phone, but not with an iPhone. If you're looking for an inexpensive way to shoot video using a mobile phone, you can try what I did. I bought two phones, but didn't activate them. I found an Android phone and a Windows Phone for $30, $15, respectively. These phones can be used for just about everything except calling.

I love that these phones can be used as a digital camera, and they have incredible storage capacities. This isn't possible currently with iPhones. If you have an Android, or

Windows Phone, you can already do it. A smartphone is also smaller than a point and click digital camera and can capture even more videos.

I'm not just saying that, but you can also download apps so I can edit the video directly on my phone. Then I can upload it to YouTube. There is no need to use a computer for editing video. While I always have my iPhone, I sometimes carry another phone to capture photos or videos. Because I haven't activated the 'video' phone, I can't upload videos unless I'm connected to Wi–Fi.

What should you include on your videos?

YouTube lets you post any video. However, you can make these videos more relevant to your business. Here are some ideas. These are just my suggestions. However, you can let your imagination run wild. YouTube is an effective marketing tool. Your video should be engaging and shared as often as possible. Your personality and humor are important.

I find videos that have a primary cameraperson on them more engaging than those that just show random footage. This person could be you, or someone you know. They don't necessarily have to be on camera for the whole thing. They don't have to be present at every stage of the video. It is important to bring life and excitement to your videos so that people can imagine what they will experience when they visit your food trucks. You can create a positive atmosphere by showing people how delicious the food will taste. Make sure the food is attractively presented and take close-up photos so that customers can see all the details. Make sure to take photos of your and your employees so they can be recognized when they are in person. Make sure to include pictures of your food truck, a product with your logo and happy customers. Remember these points when you shoot your next video.

Give Your Food Truck a Tour

YouTube video marketing has been used by many businesses to show customers their products. Food truck owners have the advantage of having many photographic opportunities. If your truck is in front of you, it can act as a background and a subtle branding cue. Food trucks can be found in many locations and are always moving. It can be fun to take a look at your truck from a distance.

If you're still building your truck, it is smart to take footage so you can show your customers. Get them excited about your launch. It's never too young to start marketing your company. Customers get to see how the food truck is progressing. If you want to look back at your journey, you can also take pictures.

Showcase Your Delicious Food

Your food is the place where your videos should generate the most buzz. Make videos for every item on the menu. The viewer should be hungry after watching your food videos. I know from personal experience that many of my favorite recipe videos made me hungry. Yours should feel the same. Photographs of people enjoying your dishes, as well as you and your staff preparing them should be taken.

However, to really make people eat your food, you should take close up shots. Make sure you take pictures of the dish in a bowl or on plates. Serve it with condiments and stir it. If the food has been wrapped in paper, you should slowly remove it from your video to reveal what's inside. For viewers to be able to see what's inside, sandwiches and wraps must be cut in half.

I need to emphasize the importance of getting close-ups of your dishes. You won't get the same effect if your video is too close to the viewers so they can't see the layers or the juiciness. A variety of close-up shots will create a video that is interesting and holds viewers' attention.

Introduce your staff members

Your staff is an important part of your business. They are the ones who will interact with your customers. A few videos featuring your staff are a good idea. So your customers can see the same face every time they go to your truck. Your customers will feel like they know the person who will be their order from because of this familiarity.

Consider including biographical information about staff members and asking them to share interesting facts about themselves. This can create a more casual interaction between your employees, customers, and vendors. It is a good idea to ask them about their interests. Do they have a pet? Include the pets in your video. Different parts of the video will appeal differently to different people. There is no need to put everything in one video. It's okay to sometimes split this information into more than one video so you can post more.

Your employees should tell you about the work they do at your food truck. These ideas are also applicable to co-owners and employees who don't have staff. I know that some of you have no employees. You must be personable, so customers recognize you and want you to meet them. You're building relationships with customers before they visit your truck.

Demonstrate the way you prepare your food

A demonstration video is another type you can create. Cooking videos are a common choice for food truck operators and others in the food-and-drink industry. It is a smart idea to show how you cook your food. The recipe doesn't have to be shared, but it might interest your customers. If you show your customers how to prepare your recipes, it can help you build a better relationship when they visit your truck. It all depends on your comfort level.

You can even create videos of your shopping trips. Imagine taking photos at a farmer's market as you pick the ingredients. Perhaps you could demonstrate how to assemble a gigantic sandwich or how garnish dishes. There are many options.

Video Recap

Make a video about the highlight of attending a special occasion. While you might not be able to take video, there are still some photos that can be used to make a slideshow. A friend could also be invited to join you at the event to take some video. Tell them that you'll provide food if they do this favour for you. Most people would not accept food for free.

This video or the photos that are shown should show the atmosphere and the location of the event. Be sure to show off your truck and what you're serving. Although it is great to show the viewers where your truck is, remember that the video is meant to promote you and your food business.

Also, thank your hosts. Don't forget to send a link out to your clients once the video is finished and uploaded to YouTube. This will allow them to share it via their social media platforms like Facebook and Twitter.

React to the Comments

YouTube allows viewers to comment under your videos. This is another area where you can interact with your customers to build a stronger relationship. You will give off the impression that others are open to you and friendly when you reply to their comments.

YouTube message alerts do not have to be enabled (I don't), but I do log on once a week to view comments and respond if necessary. This is my way to batch commenting on YouTube.

Make your channel unique

Upload a cover picture to make your YouTube channel stand out. This is the banner that appears at top of your channel pages. You will need to upload an image that is 2560x1440 pixels. However, depending on the device used to view the image, the actual size will vary. This is a strange thing to me as it appears that most of what I see in the image are cut out. The logo/text safe zones are located at the center of the 2560x1440 picture. They can be seen on all devices. However any graphic information outside the safe zones can and will still be visible on different devices.

Your next step is to group related videos together. YouTube allows you the ability to create playlists that include titles. Create a section called recipes if you have several recipe videos. You can then link to your videos in that section or playlist. The viewer will notice a cleaner channel and be more likely to subscribe if there are several sections.

Clicking the subscribe button takes you to your channel page. You may not be able to attract subscribers if your channel seems chaotic or unorganized. There are several channels that I use, but I need to make sure I only have one channel. I have about 60 videos uploaded to my channel. However, my channel page shows only 4 videos. To the viewer, it appears I have only four videos. I actually have many more. It's possible that this is part of the reason my subscriber number is slowly increasing right now.

Make your videos search engine-friendly

YouTube does not automatically know what your video is about unless you provide some assistance. YouTube can recognize your voice and create closed-captioning automatically for videos. But it's not very reliable. A detailed description is required for your video in order to increase its chances of being found by search engines like Google. This includes details such as your truck name and your city. Your videos should be tagged with keywords related your business and the content you are showing.

SEO experts advised me to include the URL for your food truck website first in your description. So it is clickable, make sure it starts with http://. Your website will be easily accessible by viewers if they wish to learn more about the food truck. This allows your followers to easily visit your website to view your full menu, see photos of your food and learn more information about you.

Chapter 8: Getting Your Food Truck Business Listed On Yelp

Yelp has the largest number of reviews for local restaurants. Up until recently, most Yelp reviews were for brick and mortar restaurants. However, more food trucks are appearing in the top reviews. This is an excellent place for your food truck's visibility. You can also rank your Yelp listing higher than your own website using search engines. Yelp results almost always rank on the first pages of Google searches when you do a search to find restaurant reviews. You can even interact with customers by leaving comments and getting ratings.

Yelp can almost work on autopilot, gathering reviews, photos and comments as well as gaining clicks for your website. Your food truck should be listed on Yelp.

First steps

Claim a Yelp listing as soon as possible. It involves filling in some details about your business using the online form. This information will need to verify, but it's easy and can be done by any business owner. The verification process includes entering a verification codes shortly after you have submitted your application. Once you've completed the verification process and claimed your business you'll be eligible to:

* Respond to posts - This is possible publicly or privately

* Track your page's views - Yelp lets you see how many views your page has and who your customers are.

* Upload photos – Submit your favourite photos that showcase your business

* Link your website - This link is crucial to drive people to your site, which will allow you to provide more content for your customers.

* Add business hours, phone number and email address. Customers want to be able get information and to contact you if needed.

Visit this website to begin the claim process:

https://biz.yelp.com/support/claiming

Below is basic information to help you get started. You can click on the button "Claim Your Business" to get started. After you have clicked that button, you will be asked to enter your business name and a postal code. You will see a few options. These may raise additional questions, which I will discuss here.

Scenario 1 – A message that says "No business Listed" is the first thing you will encounter when claiming a business. This happens if your company is just starting out or hasn't been around for a while. But don't worry. To add your business, all information regarding your business will be required.

* Types of Businesses - This is where you will organize your business into specific categories like education, professional service, or restaurants.

* Email Address

* Business Address

* Business Hours

* Business Website Address

Once you have provided the necessary information, an email will be sent to you with a confirmation. In the confirmation email, you will find a link which you must click to initiate the process. Yelp will confirm your email address. Once the request is approved, you can use your account and optimize your listing.

Scenario 2- You might see a message saying, "Already locked" If your food truck company shows up as unlocked, it is likely that someone has already taken your business. Verify that none of your coowners have claimed your company. Yelp can assist you in resolving this matter if this is an error.

Scenario #3 - This is the easiest scenario. If your business is listed in Yelp's system but has not yet been claimed, you will see the "Unlock" button. Click on the button "Unlock" next to your business name. This will unlock the page. For the unlock process to take place, you must enter your fullname, email address, create your password, and then agree to these terms and conditions.

How to Optimize Your Yelp Listing

Once you have claimed the listing, you must optimize it so that people can find it easily. This involves filling in all information about your company, adding photos, and using the analytics system. Yelp, a powerful website, can help you market your food truck company and bring customers to it. Yelp is a powerful tool that allows you to use all its features to your advantage. There are many things you can do to optimize your listing.

Enter your business information

Your business information must be completed completely. There are many fields to fill out. The more information, the better your business listing. This information will be extremely helpful to customers and profitable for your business.

Your address, phone number and hours of operation are the basics. Other details you can include are price ranges, parking availability and Wi-Fi accessibility. Outdoor seating is also possible. Credit card acceptance is another option. Although some fields may not be applicable to food trucks specifically, it is important that you complete all required fields.

You can also go back to edit the information later if you have added or changed any features. Yelp must approve any changes to take effect. They will notify you that they have received and approved your request.

Upload Photos

Everybody loves to see photos online so make sure your Yelp listing has plenty! The more photos you include, the more interesting your Yelp listing will become. When I go through a Yelp listing, I find that the photos are what really sell me about a business. Yelp's research has shown that listing that have photos get viewed 2.5 times more often than listings that don't.

Customers can also upload photos. Customers can upload photos along with comments. These photos will automatically be added to the Yelp photo galleries. Your photo gallery will grow as more people comment, review, or post photos.

Respond to Customer Comments

Yelp's whole platform is built upon user reviews. It's where people go before they visit businesses. It gives you an idea about how customers feel about the business. Keep an eye on the Yelp listings for new reviews.

Your business's attention and concern for others is demonstrated by your response to reviews and comments. You don't have to respond to every comment, but it is good practice for positive reviews.

You may occasionally receive negative reviews. These customers should always get a response. No matter how unprofessional the review, you should respond professionally. These comments can be seen by the public. Other reviewers may see your negative response and this could have an impact on future customers. Yelp is not a place to use profanity, threats or insults. Doing this will only make your business worse.

Add Keywords

It is very common to find Yelp listings in search engines like Google, Bing, and others. Like any other webpage, it is important to optimize it properly so that search engines can find it. Keywords are words that are relevant and related to your business. In this case it is your food truck.

Your keywords could include:

Crispy Cheez

Crispy Cheez food truck

Crispy Cheez Houston

Food truck serving grilled cheese

Houston food truck

Houston Grilled Cheese Sandwich

Sandwich food truck

Houston's finest grilled cheese

Mobile grilled Cheese

Grilled cheese catering

Grilled cheese restaurant

Houston Food Truck Catering

Houston Catering

Best grilled cheese

Gourmet grilled cheese

Organic grilled cheese

These are just some examples. But they should give some inspiration for your Yelp page. While you don't necessarily need to include a lot of keywords on your page, it is a good idea to have 6-8 keywords at the minimum to optimize your page for keywords.

Encourage reviews – The more reviews you have on Yelp, your business will be more established. The hardest thing to do when you start out is to get the first reviews. However, once there are some reviews, it should be much easier to build that number. Here are some tips to help you get reviews.

Link to Yahoo! - Include a button linking to Yelp in your website. People should see the Yelp logo prominently on the button so they know where it is taking them. You have a better chance of getting people to click on your button if you place it above the fold.

QR Code on Vehicle Wrap-In addition to your social media logos, you can also add a Yelp logo to the truck's exterior. You can also add a QRcode to let customers who have smartphones access your Yelp site. This doesn't necessarily have to be on your vehicle wrap. But you could also place a sticker next to the service window.

Yelp Promotions - Businesses can promote special Yelp Deals. These deals will increase the visibility of your page and can encourage customers who are there to leave reviews.

Yelp optimization - Although we have discussed optimization before, I'll repeat that properly optimized Yelp pages will attract more people. You will rank higher in search engines, which leads to more clicks and visibility.

Reviewers should not feel desperate when seeking reviews. Customers should engage rather than ask for reviews. You should create an environment where customers feel comfortable posting reviews instead of feeling obliged.

Positive reviews are great, but you can't please everybody 100% of the time. That means you'll get negative reviews eventually. You should respond quickly to negative reviews and rectify the situation. It's okay to apologize and let the customer know what you will do to fix it. You don't need to stress about negative reviews unless there are a lot. This could indicate that you have larger problems!

A few negative reviews aren't necessarily a bad thing. It's possible to look suspicious if your 5-star reviews all have 100% positive ratings. If you have positive reviews that outnumber the negative, then you should be okay. Sometimes people leave negative reviews that you can't please. Please thank them for their feedback, and move on.

Yelp's Business Owner Complaints

Yelp filters are the last thing that I want to talk. Yelp's algorithms were programmed in order to filter out fake reviews. This is a good thing. The main problem that business owners have with this is the fact that not enough good reviews are being removed, which can impact your rankings and visibility.

This is when a reviewer leaves one Yelp Review and has not filled out their profile fully. Yelp can quickly identify this pattern as suspicious, even if it's an authentic review.

If you want to remove these glowing reviews, encourage them to complete their profile fully and add reviews of other businesses that they have been to. Reviewers should inform you that their comments will not be visible if they do not complete their profile. Once they have filled out their profile, and become more active on Yelp.com, then their comments will be public and available for all to see on your Yelp page.

Yelp is an amazing marketing tool that business owners can use. It's easy to get more customers and grow your revenue if done correctly. Yelp can also hurt your business by allowing customers to leave negative reviews about you and your service. Yelp can be very influential in the restaurant sector, and you should try your best to appear good on Yelp.

Chapter 9: Customer Reward Programmes

Growing your business is all about acquiring new customers. It is no surprise that new customers require businesses to invest significant time and money. Studies show that it can cost 5 to 10 times as much to acquire a new client than to sell to a loyal customer. Research shows that customers who are already loyal spend 67% more than those who are new. It's clear that keeping customers coming back to your food truck business is a huge benefit. Mobile food markets are highly competitive. To attract and keep customers, you must be attractive and loyal to your business.

How can you keep customers returning and spending money with your company? Customer loyalty programs are the key to keeping your customers coming back. Most businesses have some kind of customer loyalty or rewards program in place to get customers to buy again.

American Airlines was the first to introduce a customer loyalty programme on a large-scale and it was widely recognized in the United States. The goal was to give passengers something special in return for flying with them. American Airlines' first frequent flyer program allowed passengers the ability to earn miles and use them on future flights. Frequent flyer programmes are now commonplace within the airline industry.

Loyalty programs are most effective for businesses that serve repeat clients. Restaurants, food trucks, and other businesses that serve repeat customers fall under this category. Customers will return if you provide great food and exceptional customer service. Recognize them for being loyal customers to keep them coming back. How many times has it happened that you have visited a restaurant and received a 11th sandwich for no cost?

Effective loyalty programs

You have probably seen a loyalty programme in many businesses you have visited. A loyalty program simply rewards customers who make regular purchases. Customers who return often to a loyalty program receive special offers, coupons, free merchandise, and gifts.

It may sound easy to set up loyalty programs, but the following facts will help you understand it. A study revealed that most households have memberships in 29 loyalty programs. But, only 12 of all the loyalty programs they have joined are active. It means that many companies invest a lot in rewards programs, but get very little or no value. You must offer value to customers by making them part of your loyalty program. How can you make your loyalty program more profitable for your food truck enterprise?

Loyalty Programme Features

Numerous companies offer loyalty programmes. There are many options. Some are straightforward, others feature-rich and sophisticated. It is crucial to select one that you believe will work well for your food truck enterprise in the long term. But you never know if your loyalty program will end or be replaced with a bigger rewards program. This fear should not stop you from creating a loyalty program.

Here are some tips and ideas that I can offer to help you find the right loyalty program. This will be a great guideline to help you get started with a loyalty program for your food truck. It is quite common to move programs around if you feel it isn't working well for you. These are some tips and features that you might want to look at.

Simple Point Systems

The point system is the oldest and most popular loyalty program. Customers who visit your truck regularly can earn points which they can redeem for rewards once they have reached a threshold. Customers can get a discount, special treatment or even free items!

These cards can be found in many forms and are familiar to everyone. Some of these cards are simply punch cards. Others use magnetic cards along with a database to keep track. The point system should be clear and easy to understand. Do not make it too complicated. You can use the term points to describe different tracking methods. One example is:

* Receive the 11th sandwich free when you purchase 10 sandwiches

* Spend $50 get your next dish free

Customers will return to your food truck more often if they make short-term purchases. They also earn points that can be used to reward them for coming back. Points can be awarded by the number of items purchased, or by the dollar amount spent.

Tier System

The balance between loyalty programs and rewarding customers for their loyalty is tricky. Customers should not have to go through lengthy processes to reach reward thresholds.

It will frustrate your customers, and it can make your loyalty program less effective. You can solve this problem by creating a tier system.

If you have a tier structure, you can reward those who sign up for your loyalty program. This encourages signing up. By increasing the value of rewards in different tiers, you can return customers. Each tier can be made more attractive by offering greater value or better rewards as they go up the ladder. Customers will be more likely to remember your loyalty programme if they are able to take less time to redeem their rewards. Customers will not remember or disregard your loyalty program if there is too much time between the reward and payout. The most important difference between a tier and a points system is that customers only receive their rewards for a short time.

Your food truck company can offer a free beverage or appetizer to the first signup for your loyalty programme. As they progress to the next tier, you can offer greater rewards, such 2 appetizers as a free gift or another reward.

How to Measure Effectiveness

Your loyalty program is not complete just because you have it in place. You should be able to assess the effectiveness of your efforts. Your loyalty program should aim to increase customer satisfaction, and keep them coming back.

Most likely, your business will use an online database that has a rewards program. These systems are great for tracking and analytics. It is possible to use a punchcard system, but it will be more difficult for you to determine its effectiveness.

Customer retention rates

Analyzing your analytics will begin with your Customer Retention Ratio. This measure measures how long customers are loyal to your company. This should increase as your loyalty program succeeds. You can add more people to the program over time. Studies have shown that a 5% increase of customer retention can translate into a 25% to 100% increase for your company's profits.

Negative Churn

Churn is something you might have heard. Churn is the rate at which your customers stop doing businesses with you. If I use the term negative churn it means that customers are spending more money with you. Negative churn can be used to counter the natural phenomenon where customers leave your business.

Net Promoter Score

The net promoter score measures customer satisfaction and whether they would recommend your business. This is often a scale from 1-10, with 10 being most popular. The net promoter scores are calculated by subtracting the percentages of detractors and promoters from your business.

The fewer people you have to detract from, the better. A net promoter rating of 70% or more is considered good. You can reach this number by having a great loyalty programme. Sending surveys to customers is a great way to increase customer satisfaction. These surveys can usually be done online and sent as notifications through your loyalty program.

When is it a good idea to create a loyalty programme?

Loyalty program can be launched at any time in your business. Many businesses that are older have been in the business of running it for years before creating a loyalty programme. They may have had to start from scratch without reliable systems, but now they realize the advantages of having them.

Some start a loyalty programme right from the beginning. Here's a suggestion. You can get onboard a loyalty program that suits your business if you haven't yet launched your food truck. This will help you to launch your food truck. This way, when you launch your truck you can immediately start customers on your loyalty programme. Start a special event to launch your truck and let customers learn about the program.

You can also cater events and gather signups from multiple people in one location. Catering events offer guests the opportunity to spend more time with your business and you. Remember to bring your loyalty program to any event.

I'm not able to cover all loyalty programs for businesses in this book. However, I can list some so you have a good starting place to search for the best one. You won't be able to choose the right one. However, I hope the information provided in this chapter will help guide you.

Here is a brief list to get your started. These companies are subject to change and may cease to exist at any time.

* Belly

* Square

* LevelUp

* FiveStars

* Wali

* Perka

* SpotOn

* PunchCard

* SpendGo

* Swipley

* FourSquare

Most of the rewards programs listed above, if they are not all, use mobile apps and electronic tracking to make it easy to track your customers' reward status. This lets customers know when they will be able to receive a reward and can encourage them back to visit.

Customer Reward Programs

Different business types offer different rewards. You can increase your chances of providing a positive customer experience by following these guidelines. Experts suggest expanding your reach beyond simply offering discounts on goods. This is because discounts don't make a lasting impression with customers. Rewards with tangible items are much more popular than plain discounts. It's easy to speak directly to customers when you work in the food truck industry.

If you want to create your own rewards program, it is worth copying other successful programs. Also, consider offering something new. For more information, research brick-and–mortar restaurants, bakeries ice cream shops, food truck owners, and other businesses to learn about their operations. To see their programs in action and to learn more about the types of benefits they offer, sign up. Ask yourself if the rewards offered are fair and interesting.

Make sure you choose the program that best reflects what you've experienced. A service you sign-up for is also a key factor in how your rewards programs work. Some features are more extensive than others. You may not need all features. Cost and fees will also play a role. The ones that you aren't able to afford or feature you don't want or need will be removed. Your customers want to be able enjoy the rewards. To ensure that they don't forget it, it is best for them to be in a position to redeem the award every 3 to6 months. This will stimulate them to return to your store and buy more. Customer loyalty programs should not take too much time for them to see results from their business. A customer will lose interest if they do not see the value.

It is well-known that loyalty programs are a highly effective marketing tool. These programs, when implemented properly, can increase profits as well as keep customers coming back. Loyalty programs are a great way to increase your brand's awareness and your reputation. Research the available loyalty programs to help you plan your implementation. This is an opportunity you don't want missed!

FOOD TRUCKING BUSINESS

A

Food trucks are a great way to make money as people often eat at mobile restaurants. Instead of waiting to see if customers will come to your restaurant, you can direct them to your location and show them delicious food.

You can start and run a food truck business with much less staff than what you would need to manage a traditional restaurant. It is also much more affordable than traditional eateries and has lower overheads.

It's better to get started with a reasonable business arrangement. You will need to choose a specialty for your food business. Choose the dishes that you would like to serve and the customers you want to target. These elements will impact the most important aspects and functions of your business. You must choose them early on. You must decide whether your business will sell fast food, icecream, soups, pastries or multi-cuisine food. The age range you want to target is important as well. This includes teens, children, executives and senior citizens. Even though there might be overlaps between age groups, you must ensure your target clients are at top of your priority lists before you can launch your business.

Also, it is important to set a goal that is at the top rank of your priority list. Consider, for example, where will your business be in the next five or ten year? How many additional trucks and employees would you require at that time? What type of income are you looking for in the future, and what is it? These are some goals you must set at the outset for your business.

If you have a clear idea of your goals and objectives, you can then start to get the licenses and permits you need. Know which cities and towns do not allow food trucks to operate. The laws of the area will determine the location you choose for your business.

You will need to get a food truck license once you have them. You can purchase a used or new truck or lease one for a certain time. If your business requires subsidization, you will need to find a reliable bank or private investor.

All of these things will allow you to immediately start your business. You must be unique and offer nothing else to succeed in the mobile-food business. Individuals seek novelty and variety constantly. Food Trucks will be a success if they deliver exactly what they are looking for.

Why should you consider a food truck operation?

A popular way to make money in the restaurant industry is through the concessions business. There are many reasons to get into this business before opening a permanent restaurant. A versatile concession business requires fewer investments. You can make a name for yourself among the local population. Because the business is portable, you can visit different locations before you settle on one. In the aftermath of opening your own food concessions, you may decide that you want to keep it forever, start a restaurant without it, or make it the restaurant you long for.

There are a few reasons to prefer a flexible food concession company over a brick and mortar business. It is riskier to start a business in the food sector if you don't have any previous industry experience. A restaurant owner is something that you will need to do at all times. It's a wonderful way to start small and build your way to the top. This type is easier to manage and control than just bouncing into one of the 75-seat restaurants. A food truck may have many dollars to spend. However, conventional eateries can easily reach a large amount of dollars. These are just a few examples of practicality. If your business fails to succeed, you will have contributed less.

One reason you might sell food at a concession stand is the freedom to create a local company. You can use the concession trailer to help you get funds if you don't have the cash immediately to invest in a restaurant. In addition to offering locals benefits, you also get to know the people. If you have regular clients who frequent another restaurant with the same name, your concession business will draw rehash customers.

The best part about a food truck is that it can be easily transported, so you can go to another place if you don't like the one you have. Many times, conventional restaurants are not able to find great business. Even though you have the perfect location, great food, excellent management, and a lot more pedestrian activity than the average restaurant, it won't get the salary it needs. A static restaurant can't do much other than surrendering or sticking it out. In any event, the main advantage of a trailer or versatile truck is that it can be moved wherever money is available.

While owning your own restaurant may be a dream come true for many people, it isn't always possible. Start your own food concession business. This is an easier, cheaper and more useful way to get started in this industry. These and many other reasons show that starting a concession truck is an intelligent idea.

How can I be sure I've found the most successful food truck business?

You may not find a person offering a meal on the target in the same industry. Do some research to find the right mobile truck food business. You don't need another concession business. Or, would you prefer to run a food concession with a fresh and unique menu that's uninfluenced by others?

Since you want to earn money, it is a good idea to start your own business. Picking the right activity is key to success. A reliable mobile food truck platform will provide all the resources, tools, devices, and tools necessary to ensure that you are able to quickly and effectively get out of the gate. You'll make many mistakes and take wrong turns if this is something you do on your own. Are you sure you have enough money and the ability to make it work? Look for an industry leader that has a training program in place and frameworks in place to save you years and much trial and error.

The best mobile food business plans are well-constructed and designed to draw in clients from a diverse population. They offer training right away and support you for as long or short as you need.

Mobile food concessions are now offering healthier options, such as hand-tapped Vermont beef patties and a range of wraps. They have been able to grow exponentially and continue to surpass expectations even in difficult economic times. If you are able to work with top mobile concessions franchises, your mobile food business will thrive. Your staff will have amazing experiences serving clients with a range of interesting and healthy options. It's impossible to make mistakes in a tight environment. Your training equips you with the necessary plans and food preparation conventions to meet your customers' expectations. Your training's state-of-the art online detailing frameworks and support team mean that you won't have long to manage paperwork.

HOW TO MAKE YOUR BUSINESS SMART

A

Once you and your partner have decided what roles to play and how much profit to share, you need to start drafting the business plan. This is where the big idea will take shape. We'll first discuss the key points and important details that your business plans will require. Next we'll look at an example business plan.

What is a Business plan? Why is it important?

Businesses need business plans to be eligible for third-party financing from banks, small businesses administrations, and other lenders.

Even though you may not be required to make one, preparation and planning are vital to the success your business. They will save you money and help you avoid making costly mistakes.

Even if there are partners, the business plan plays a critical role in ensuring alignment of vision. This is necessary to avoid any disputes later that may threaten the survival of the business.

Here are some things to consider when planning a food truck business

You should plan for certain items that are specific to food trucks, such as:

The Local Food Truck Marketplace

This is one of most difficult decisions to make as it requires lots of objective data, gathered from primary and secondary sources.

In this instance, we would like to open a food truck operation. You may need to do some industry research or statistics, but it's best to familiarize yourself with local brands. This will include internet research to find out about food trucks in your region (to help with differentiation, branding).

Also, look out for "foodtruck lots". Many cities have lots that are leased for a fleet of trucks. These spaces are often used by food trucks that park permanently. They also offer predictability, something many food truck business lack. This location is likely to be the best for your new business. You'll have documented foot traffic, predictable food prices, and fairly consistent sales, something that is very rare in this industry. There is a potential downside to this, however. Your brand will need be significantly different from the other trucks' offerings.

It is also worthwhile to search for local fairs, festivals, or events within 50-miles of your home. These information can be found online and organizers often offer exhibitor and attendance information to help you get there. This information is useful for projecting costs and demonstrating to potential investors the areas where you intend to seek revenue.

Understanding the Competition

Once you have looked at the local markets, you'll need to find trucks that are either directly or indirectly competing with the truck you created. Direct competition would mean a menu offering substantially similar to the one that you are thinking of. You want to make sure that you don't set yourself up for competition with a well-known brand in a specific market. Some overlap in the menu could be considered indirect competition. However, the menus had enough variation that clients could choose to visit both businesses even if they were in the same place. You might consider changing your menu to decrease concerns about indirect and direct competition.

Food trucks' success depends on their ability to differentiate themselves from the competition.

This does not mean you should start a food cart similar to one in the region, but it does say that you should only do this after you have determined how you intend to compete against that truck.

Sometimes, however, the strategy that will lead to success is more complex than that.

Can you provide better quality food or longer service hours? Or maybe a combination of both?

Business Strategy

You can use four business approaches to increase your chance of success in business planning. These include cost leadership, differentiation and location.

Cost Leadership Strategy

This strategy is often what a new business looks for, and can prove to be very costly. You should not consider it unless you have exceptional circumstances. This is not a good idea if you have a highly-trafficked food product. You can still make a profit if you're selling hot dogs or hamburgers at the state fair, for example. Further research is needed to find the lowest food cost and quality at which you can live. It is not enough to be cheap to build repeat customers. If you don't be careful, your customers may think that your food is of lower quality and less attractive to them.

Differentiation Strategy

Differentiation is the next strategy. It's also the most common. The differentiation strategy would allow your food truck to only sell unique food products. These products can be family secrets, difficult-to find food products, or new dishes. They set you apart from the rest. Although quality is crucial in the differentiation strategy, high-quality, hard-to-find food products can lead to greater margins for your brand, which will result in higher profits and less work. This will impact your overall business value and result in higher returns on investments.

Location Strategy

This can be a very profitable strategy, especially for the first food truck. It will also ensure that you have a loyal customer base. This is what a truck-owner in Los Angeles does. He learned from a local clothing manufacturer that there were hundreds of employees. Many of these people did not have cars. He asked the owner if they could offer breakfast and lunch to the employees and pay a small percentage to the company in return for permission to set up shop there. The truck started to move and is now permanently based there. An additional truck was bought in the next few months for growth. This strategy can be extremely effective if you have a local area with few restaurants or employees who are unable to go for lunch.

Hybrid Strategy

This strategy employs a combination or all of the approaches above to maximize the success rate of the truck. We may know of trucks that stop at a place every Monday, another every Tuesday, etc. This can lead to increased brand loyalty by causing customers to feel a sense of urgency when they know that they will not be able get the item on a certain day. This combination would bring together both differentiation and location while also spreading awareness about the brand.

For festivals or events with high traffic, others might offer a completely different menu.

Food Pricing

It is crucial that you decide the price of your product before you start putting together a business strategy. For food trucks, there are many ways to price your products correctly so that your product appeals to your target market. It is important to consider the price of raw materials when determining the cost of the dish.

Most restaurants will charge between 35 and 45 percent of the dish's total cost. This would include food, plates, garnishes, and forks. Imagine that you have a dish with ingredients costing $5. You could make it as expensive as $7.25. You can experiment with pricing. Price can be a factor in driving up costs. Exclusion can cause costs to rise. Baseball stadiums, for instance, may charge $6 for a $2 hotdog. People who eat lunch on weekdays are more likely to pay higher prices than people who attend festivals.

Pricing your products too low can send a message to your customers that the food quality is poor. Explore your options and find the right price range for each item.

If there are other trucks nearby, you should take the time and walk around the site to get an idea of the prices and what their offers are. When all other vendors are charging $2 for water, don't charge $4 for a bottle.

Also important when pricing your items is labor. This applies to both preparation in the kitchen, and service from the truck. You may adjust the price for items that are more labor-intensive than others in your menu.

Failing to do so can result in a lackluster profit that discourages the owner and lowers the chances of the truck succeeding.

Strategic Partnerships

The business plan should include strategic partnerships. An extremely successful lobster roll brand relies on a family fishing link to provide an affordable product that can easily be marked up for an impressive margin. This example shows how a supplier strategic partnership can be a competitive advantage. The business will be more attractive for financing and increase its chances of success. Strategic alliances could also include exclusive lease rates or favorable lease terms offered by festival organizers, who may share a small portion of the profits. It is worthwhile to think about the people you know and how they can help you gain competitive advantage.

Also, even if your supplier network is not established, it's important that you spend significant time talking to and sampling food vendors. This will allow you to negotiate price, assure product quality, and reduce hard costs. To demonstrate that you are ready to succeed to investors, your efforts in this area should be documented in a business plan.

As you grow more experienced and get involved with other events, it is important that you keep in touch with the organizers of previous events. There are many organizers in this field. They can offer you great opportunities to locate suitable locations and provide advance notice.

This can be a great way to make your brand famous, regardless of whether you give money to a cause that's being covered in the media or offer unusual food that's newsworthy. There are many food trucks offering food challenges. One example is a 8-pound burrito that can be eaten by two people in less than one hour. These stories are not expensive, but they provide a compelling story. Many news outlets love these human interests to fill in the gaps when slow news isn't available.

Food Truck Business Pros and Con

Pros

These are the benefits of operating a food truck:

Very small initial investment

The food truck business is not expensive to start. This is unlike a walk-in or rented place.

The only thing that could cost you the most money in the trucking business is the purchase of a truck, and any equipment. A good truck can be found for a bargain price, or your family might have one in great condition that you could use. This will allow you to save time and money on buying a truck.

Minimum Risk

The risks involved in the food truck industry are lower than those in other businesses. This business is very safe as you have little chance of losing your money.

A Short Time After Opening the Business, More Customers

Foods sold from a food truck are usually cheaper than those purchased in restaurants. It's affordable. A typical man can afford a meal at a food truck. A good number of people will come to you if your services cost-effective.

Before you begin, you can build your brand.

The food truck business allows you to build your brand before you even venture into the full-fledged market. Your brand is what sells your business. So as a food truck operator, you already know what makes up your business, the special meals you offer and how you intend to promote them. A food truck, unlike other companies, is not built from scratch.

Mobility

You can move your food truck business around easily. There are some drawbacks to starting a food truck business.

Cons

Finding the Right Truck for You is a difficult task

It may be difficult to find a truck or cart that is compatible with your food truck venture. There are two options: you can get trucks that aren't strong enough and/or not big enough. Unless you have a great source, good ones are hard to come by. You might end up driving your car down to a mechanic shop from time to time.

Your car may break down

Trucks and cars will not let you know when they are going to crash. Your truck might not be able to handle the stress of driving to a high-sales location. To ensure that your vehicle is safe and sound, you should perform a routine maintenance check.

Customers are available

Your expectations may be wrong for the first few weeks or months. Because there is not enough customers for the foods you sell, your sales might drop for the next week. You should conduct a thorough study of the prospects for survival of your local food company.

Unhealthy Competition

This could lead to some setbacks for your business. You should avoid other food trucks that offer the same type of food as yours. Any competitor could take down your business at any cost. Don't sell the same foods as other food trucks. Instead, create your own menu.

FINANCIAL ESSENTIALS

W

No matter how much experience you have with small business management, the task of keeping track and achieving profitability can seem daunting. You have many options for accounting software that will simplify your finances. Intuit has QuickBooks for small business owners, and it is available from Intuit. A few online videos can help you refresh and improve your bookkeeping skills. High quality CRM and POS software for small businesses can accurately record your sales and provide valuable resources when managing employees or customers.

After you have secured financing to purchase your truck, equipment, and paid the fees associated with setting up a legal food truck company, all of these things will be possible.

Your initial funding must cover your startup's monthly costs and last at least two months to ensure that you continue to bring in income.

First, it's tempting to put all your earnings back in your business. But we advise you to resist that temptation. Keep your head on the payroll, and make sure you have an emergency fund. Then, invest in products, services, and marketing opportunities. Also, it is important not to be afraid of loans that can help you get your company off the ground. A well-planned billing strategy will help you maintain your good credit score and pay your bills on time. It is important to note that the amount of your initial loans can impact the length of time it takes for them to be paid off.

Consider your repayment plan too as you will need funds from your food truck business to cover these costs. It is vital to ensure that your expenses are covered beyond salaries and ingredients when setting your menu prices. While it is important to offer competitive pricing to your customers, you need to consider a cashflow strategy in order for your business to succeed.

Let's get started. We will explore the different options for funding your startup. Look into local opportunities. Small business loans may be a better alternative to crowdfunding campaigns due to tax incentives. Before you apply for any loans, make sure that your executive summary is ready and polished. Investors will often want to meet and interview you. To boost your confidence and to convince investors that you are serious about making your food truck financially viable, it's a smart idea to spend the time to prepare your business plan.

Lending and Financing

Online loan aggregators are able to match loan options to meet your needs. You will likely need a combination of many financing options. There are different types of financing available to food trucks. Some may be more suitable than others. Many online loan aggregators offer loans that traditional banks are unable to offer. They take into account more than your business credit score (which they will not have yet), and often offer lower minimum amounts.

Credibly or LendingTree will give you an overview of all the options available for a trim business loan, but many lenders are highly recommended for food truck entrepreneurs. LendingTree's ValuePenguin can help you find specific small business loans. You can search by the amount that you need, the credit score of your company, as well as the type and age, of your business. It saves a lot time searching for the right loan and avoids wasted effort trying to find them. There are three types of loans: for startups, expansions and businesses with poor credit. PayPal and Square are excellent options for smaller loans of one year to provide working capital in the initial months. This route is recommended if you have an existing payment processor.

A general overview might say that Crest Capital is a good option for you if your goal is to lease your truck. National Funding might work better for buying a new truck. LoanBuilder, LightStream and other lenders can help you find a loan that suits your needs. You might have a different situation. If your credit rating is not perfect, lenders such as OnDeck and Fora Financial may be able to provide a short-term loan.

Keep in mind that the best loan will depend on what your circumstances are. We have given you many options, but it's possible to find another lender that makes more sense for you. A local bank, for example, may be more inclined to lend a small amount to support a local company. Loan applications take time, and they require work. Be sure to organize all your documents before you apply to avoid costly mistakes.

Equipment Financing

Larger commercial equipment (including appliances and vehicles) that is used by businesses may be eligible for financing at lower interest rates, as the equipment serves as collateral. The truck, as well as the important appliance components of the truck can be financed in this manner. When deciding between new or refurbished equipment you should consider depreciation, as with personal vehicles.

You might be wondering where to find equipment loans. It might surprise some people that the answer is generally provided by the company that sells or resells the equipment. Although banks may offer equipment financing, this can slow down the application process. Some companies operate solely as equipment financers. Others work as online lenders. These include Balboa Capital. Currency Finance. Crest Capital. CIT.

Equipment financing can be a great option for food truck companies to pay as little as possible for overhead costs. This financing process is quick, and it offers low-interest rates. These rates are kept low by the collateral that is the equipment. This could mean your truck could be taken out of service if you default on payments. Equipment financing lenders place less importance on credit. This option is available for companies who do not have the necessary credit scores to be eligible to receive other loans.

Many lenders offering equipment financing offer equipment leases, often with the option to purchase after the lease term is over. Similar to personal vehicles, the process of equipment leasing works nearly exactly the same as with personal vehicles. Leasing is more expensive than equipment financing at 5%. It tends to be closer to 12%.

In equipment financing, it is important to consider that technological advances may quickly render your equipment obsolete. It's important not to continue using old equipment, particularly if you have a new menu or are trying to capitalize on the latest trends. Also, some equipment financing is subject to a 10% down payment. In these cases, you'll need to find another investor and lender.

A valid driver's license and voided checks for your business account are required. You also need bank statements that go back at most three months. Your credit score is necessary. These requirements can vary depending upon who is financing the equipment. Before you start any application, be sure that you have all of the information you require.

Microloans for Businesses

There are many small business loan opportunities available. But, you should start by looking at the websites of the federal government. SBA 7a loans or other microloans specific to small businesses in the United States are any loan below $50,000. This is much less than most banks can offer. Because they allow for flexibility, these are ideal for small business. Although it takes longer to apply, these funds can be used for working capital, inventory, supplies or equipment. This could allow you to finance multiple financial requirements with one loan.

SBA loans are technically subcategories within the larger grouping microloans. They are specifically intended for access to those who are underserved. Opportunity Fund is one such example. They serve primarily minority-owned and women-owned small business owners, as these entrepreneurs often lack access to traditional loan opportunities. Many microlenders target small-business owners, so it's possible to find a microlender that best suits your needs. It is important to understand the requirements for microloans. In some cases, you will be required to provide collateral or guarantee the loan amount.

Lines of Business Credit

In order to set up your business or repay a credit line, you might need working capital. The ability to borrow capital at your own pace, as opposed to borrowing in advance, allows you to open a line of credit. The exact amount of capital required to start a food truck business is unknown. Approval for a significant amount allows you to use your credit when you need it, such as if equipment financing is unavailable for a grill to be started.

Your monthly payments will be similar to a creditcard, but your credit limit can be much higher, depending on terms and credit rating. The credit limit can range between $10,000 and $1,000,000. If you don't plan to use it immediately, it is worth opening a line business credit. You should always have the option of having it in case you ever need it. A timely repayment is a great option if your goal is to build good credit for business.

Business Credit Cards

These cards are useful for small businesses even though they come with shorter repayment terms and higher interest rates. Every business will have to pay unexpected costs or cover last-minute emergencies. A credit card is able to help in this situation. You might be able to benefit from introductory or reward offers by choosing a business card. You might consider a card with travel-related bonuses if you travel frequently with your truck. These cards are another way to build good credit. The terms and conditions of your card will be important to you. Set up electronic payments to make sure you don't miss any payments or damage your credit score. The types of food truck purchases you plan on using the card for will determine the rewards that it offers.

Major credit card companies offer credit options for businesses. Chase, American Express, Capital One all offer affordable rates for small businesses.

Cash Flow & Expenses

The cost of starting a business can be expensive. You will need to learn how to finance your startup costs before your food truck idea is realized. The "fun" part of this business is menu planning and designing your truck. Although running a food cart can be fun, it's still a business that must be managed. Although looks can be deceiving, the process of opening a food truck business is much like starting a regular restaurant. It's not an easy way to become a successful business. You will need to work hard and dedicate your time to survive in this business.

Your cash flow is crucial to your success. This is possible through smart supply purchasing and proper pricing. Also, you should be very careful with your expenses. There is no set cost to start a gourmet food cart business. Each food truck has unique needs. Begin by listing every expense you can think about. You won't be surprised to see how quickly your costs increase. This will allow you to estimate the costs of producing each dish. This is vital because it gives you an idea of the cost of each dish. Remember to include legal, accounting, as well as other financial expenses.

Operating Expenses

Another aspect of the equation are operating expenses. Operating expenses refer to the ongoing costs of running your business. Operational expenses can also be referred to as recurring monthly payment. This can be further broken down to give us fixed and varied expenses. You can think of vehicle payments, vehicle rentals and vehicle maintenance as fixed expenses. Insurance, web hosting, commissaries, and vehicle payments are just a few examples. Variable expenses may include ingredients, fuel and repairs, marketing, as well as special permits. It's crucial to be able accurately calculate your monthly costs. For the unanticipated, you may need to plan a bit more. Unexpected expenses can arise from last-minute events and vehicle repairs.

Your business may not be profitable immediately. It can be frustrating to watch the money disappear and not see any return on your initial investment. The longer it takes to pay back your initial investment, as the greater its value. A food truck's advantage is its lower overhead cost. Although you will need to have enough capital in order to run the food truck for six months to one year, it is possible to start up again. It can take businesses up to two years for profits to be seen, according studies. It seems like an eternity to most people.

Managing Food Volume

It will be necessary to effectively manage the quantity of food. Here are some variables that will affect the volume. This includes how much food will you buy and how much will you make. Next, think about how you are going to market your products. Calculating volume can be complex. It is possible to estimate volume at the beginning of your project to get an approximate figure. However, only experience can help you determine how much you should buy and prepare.

Figuring out how much food you can bring to a dinner service is the constant problem. This is dependent on how much food you think you can sell. This is often the case until you run out. Even worse, you may not realize how much food could be sold when you run out of food. This can be very frustrating.

Because you aren't open every day like a traditional eatery, you may have a limited amount of time to sell your food. You should be able to sell food quickly and increase sales. Pricing your menu is also important. You must have a balanced pricing policy. If your prices too high, you won't sell many products. If your fees don't meet the minimum requirements, you will not make any sales. The average price of most food truck items is $6 to $10, although some charges more.

Building loyal customers

A truck must have affordable prices to attract a large following. Comparing similar products with others is a good way to find out the price of your competitor's items. Experience is another advantage in charging the right price. You can influence the price your customers pay by considering their location. Pricing in one area will be slightly different than in another. Price is also determined by how much you eat.

You must identify what makes your food better than the rest. If you charge more than your competition, you must explain why.

Here are some ways you can charge more than your competitors for their food. You might use organic ingredients or offer side dishes not offered by other competitors. The portion size could be larger. It could be that you are using import components. It is possible to charge more for gluten-free options. It is important to remember that if your expenses are higher than your income, you will need to make adjustments.

Some adjustments that you can make include lowering your supply costs, getting bulk discount for your ingredients and adjustments to employees. You could also join a cooperative or enhance your marketing strategies. Once you've determined your costs and calculated how many items are needed to breakeven, you can then determine the amount of products that you need to sell.

It's going to be difficult for you to become financially successful in your first year. Most adjustments will be made in the first year. Of course, you can't control some things like:

* Bad weather

* Event cancellations

* Health concerns

* Vehicle breakdowns

It's all part the business. Every industry has the same problems. It's possible to persevere through some of the most difficult parts in the startup process if you have patience.

HOW TO FIND RIGHT TRUCK

T

You probably start to wonder, "Where do you find food trucks for sale?" It used to be that you couldn't find one on the newspaper classifieds. If you didn't know anyone who was retiring or who needed a stand upgrade, or if the trailer was too old, you either bought the shell of a truck and spent all of the money to get it ready to go.

Today's food truck entrepreneur is fortunate to have two incredible things going for him: the internet, and the rise of the food truck.

It is almost like shopping for your car when you shop for food trucks. There are many different makes and models available. Nearly all have some customization. Although most of them have the necessary elements, some models may not be able to meet your requirements.

If you're looking to buy an entire truck, look for a clean title and no history of major accidents. Food trucks don't have a Carfax-type program. You will need questions like, "Has the truck been on fire before?" or, "What damage was caused by it?" Are there any traffic accidents that have been very serious? or "When was the last time you had a major traffic accident?"

It would be helpful if you considered all aspects of the truck. Some of my friends have described managing their food truck like being "equal parts auto mechanic and building contractor" and they aren't wrong. But, if you don't feel confident assessing the mechanical soundness or any of these elements, take some time to get help, at least until the end of the purchase process. Hidden damage and other issues can quickly ruin your plans to run a food truck empire. An expert can quickly identify these problems and recommend repair options to save you a lot.

Let's examine the various food service vehicles available and what you need to look out for when shopping.

Pushcarts

The job of a pushcart driver is far easier.

Structural soundness is your first priority. All wheels should turn freely and move at the same pace. The axels need to be sturdy and strong enough to support the cart. Heating elements should heat, but cooling features should be kept cool. Drains and bins should be accessible and should not be covered with rust.

There are many ways to update cosmetic features without too much stress. It is possible to change exterior paint colors to reflect your brand. A menu is a must. If the pushcart is equipped with an umbrella, sunshade, or awning they can be easily replaced if necessary.

Pushcarts typically don't require a lot of wiring, pipe, or other power-operated options. If you do see these features on the cart, check to make sure that everything is working properly and there are no leaks.

You have to figure out how you will get it there. You will need to either load it into a heavy-duty pickup truck bed or trailer. Are you able to pedal it, even if it is attached to a bike, to the places you intend to store it, or will it require assistance to move it along roads and up hills?

Trailers

Concession trailers can prove tricky as many are retrofitted using empty trailers. Buyers rarely have the ability to determine who was responsible for the work and whether it was done properly. Professional evaluations are necessary for hidden elements like floor reinforcement, gas fixtures, and electrical wiring.

Many food truck entrepreneurs find it tempting to purchase a brand new trailer and customise it. This plan comes with many benefits. You can choose the items you want and have peace of mind knowing it is all right. This plan does not come without its problems. This plan is generally more expensive as you will need to purchase new fixtures, equipment, and possibly pay for their installation. A lot of skilled engineers and contractors also make their living renovating and updating food trucks. You must budget properly for the professional services you will need.

If you do decide to build it, you will need plenty of tools, lots of space and money as well as a place that is weatherproof to store the trailer while it's being constructed. You will have a memorable and profitable trailer if your skills and knowledge are strong. You might end up paying more for your trailer if you don't have the right skills.

Before you make the leap to purchase a used trailer, there are a few things you need to know.

* What is a trailer's weight limit? What is the current trailer weight and how will it change once you add any generators/propane tanks/other equipment needed for your particular business?

* How are they going to transport it from one location into another?

* Is it structurally sound Walls, floors, ceiling, etc.

* How old are these appliances? Who installed them

* Do the sinks and drains, ventilation fans, lights, gas jets, etc. work correctly? Are they working correctly? If the current owner uses "there's no trick to this", you instinctively need to back off slowly.

* Has there been an accident in the trailer, or in traffic?

* Has the trailer had a recent fire inspection.

* How many tires do you need? When were they last replaced

It is possible to be willing to compromise or overlook certain elements. However, it all depends on your budget as well as your abilities to make necessary repairs and adjustments. A trailer could be perfect, but you'd prefer to have a fridge in the pantry. This swap can be relatively simple. It will take a lot more work to find a trailer with all the things you need and love in perfect condition. However, it might be worth the effort to rewire the entire electric system. If this sounds like something you would like to tackle, it is up to you.

Trucks

Everything you have read about trailers can also be applied to trucks. Trucks are equipped with their own motors so there is no need to worry about how they will get to gigs, unless you have a natural lemon. Consider having some expertise in automobiles when considering truck options. Your car breaking down can be extremely inconvenient and potentially dangerous. It can also lead to high repair costs. If your food truck crashes on the way to a gig you have many other concerns, such as lost wages, food waste and a bad reputation for slacking at gigs. Unless you or someone within your circle are a skilled gearhead, mechanical soundness will be the most important priority for your investment.

Structural Soundness goes hand in hand with mechanical soundness. You may recall how the chuck wagons of old were reinforced to withstand the extra weight. This principle has not been changed. You can drive this vehicle on paved roads or in grassy areas. You don't have it to be off-road, but it should handle some bumps and mud.

Inside you will have the same checklist of concerns as the trailer or pushcart. Everything must work. You don't have to worry about corrosion, rust or rodents. But it can be quite difficult if your goal is to make things work. Some appliances can be modified and replaced to better suit your business. But, it's possible to find a truck which doesn't require as much modification.

The question is, where can you find these trailers, trucks, and pushcarts in the first place? I recommend looking at every online resource. I know of a few people who have had great success using online marketplaces such eBay or Craigslist. It may be necessary to travel to another place to view your prospects, but you might reconsider the "mobile food vending" idea. Like shopping for a car, it is important to examine a variety of options and compare features. You also need to weigh the challenges and benefits.

The amount of capital needed to open a food-truck depends on the case. Will you borrow money? What type of vehicle are you purchasing? To pull the trailer, do you need a vehicle? Is the food van already set up?

Prices vary depending on the area you live in and when it is. The peak season is usually when owners sell. The market is saturated with offers, and there is usually less demand since buyers won't be using the food truck for the following season. Even if you aren't planning to use your food trucks immediately, it is still a good time to purchase because you can negotiate modest prices. According to our experience, the cost to start a food cart in WA ranges from $15,000 up to $100,000. It's easy to get everything set up for under $20,000. If you make a good deal with your partner and have the necessary resources, it is possible. But if you would like a customized food truck delivered to you, you can at least multiply this amount by five!

Get started with your venture by finding the funds

Here are some tips to help you get the cash you need.

* Crowdfunding - There are many crowdfunding websites where you can post your project and draw investors from all over the world. We're talking about Fund Me, Indiegogo, Kickstarter and Fund Me. The majority of these platforms require a percentage from the amount you collect and are only available for a specific time. For strangers to consider investing their money, your project must be exciting and consistent. It would be great if you also offered prices for people who donate money to Kickstarter. PayPal's crowdfunding platform was also launched recently. The platform is meant to be free. These platforms are available for more information. Choose the one that best suits your needs!

* You can get a loan from the bank. Your banker will require a business plan. This will allow you to obtain the loan approval. It is very difficult to get loans for food trucks in Australia. A few people had their requests for loans rejected to purchase a food truck. Banks are not as open to the fact that the market is instabilized and that the activity is unstable.

* Family members and friends: You may also ask family members or friends to support your food truck, if they are willing.

* Our experience. We had worked for a time in Australia and were able to save enough to be able to fund the project ourselves without needing to borrow money. We each had $20,000 available to spend on this project. You're likely to know that even the most important jobs in Australia are well-paid. If you work 40 to 60 hours, your earnings could range from $700 to $1,000 per week. A waiter job in a restaurant can make you as much as $20 to $25 an hr. If you are willing and able to work many hours, it is possible to save a lot of

money. The cost of living and wages aren't the same in all cities. If you can control your spending and earn a good salary, you may be able to open your food truck within months if you join a group.

Looking for a Food Truck?

Gumtree helped us find our trailer. This is the largest marketplace in the country, and you will find almost all food trucks or trailers on it. You can also use Facebook's marketplace, which grows exponentially. Or you can look at Facebook groups that are dedicated to food trucks owners.

Buy an Established Business

Sometimes owners decide to sell their entire food truck business. You take over their recipes, their customers, and their social media. You can't buy a business already established and start from scratch. This option is typically more expensive than starting from scratch. But if you have the funds and the numbers they provide, you can jump right in! This option is also a good choice if you don't want all the work involved in building your food truck and decorating it. Since the previous owner did everything, there is almost nothing left to do. But, if your idea is to be developed, we recommend you buy a blank>>food truck. Although this can be a longer process, it is worth it. It won't be easy to break into the industry. You'll need to put in some effort. However, it can be motivating and beneficial to have your own business and try your hand at developing your ideas. The minimum price for a food truck was $50,000, which we couldn't afford. We also wanted our menu, and our concept. The best solution was to use a trailer to set it up!

You can buy a used or new food truck.

The decision will depend on your budget, and what your goals are for your food truck. It is possible to find a significant difference in prices between a new and second-hand vehicle in Australia.

* Buying new food trucks: A new foodtruck will give you greater safety, both from a mechanical standpoint and in terms of materials durability. You should remember that new vehicles have a substantial depreciation. This means that they will lose a large portion of their value once they are used. Also, you may not be able to sell them at the same amount you bought them. A new food truck is more susceptible to depreciation than a used one. We reached out and got quotes from companies that specialize building custom-made food truck.

* Buying second-hand food trucks: A second-hand foodtruck will require some effort to adapt to your particular project (buying appliances to match the type or menu you wish to serve), but it will be much more affordable to buy. You might also be able sell it easier! This is the solution we decided on based upon our budget and our project.

Costs of equipment for an empty food truck

We bought the trailer from an Indian restaurateur who was using it for his events. It was already fully equipped and met most security standards. It already had a fridge, microwave, and stainless steel benches. Also, the electric system was already in place. This helped us reduce the cost of our equipment. We were unable to adapt it as we desired because the inside was not designed well.

A food truck that is empty will cost you more money and time than it costs to build. All necessary items will need to be installed to meet standards. This includes an electric system for lighting and appliances, sinks and plumbing systems, venting system for the roof, isolation materials for the walls, floors and appliances.

Fitting out the trailer and decorating it cost us around $7,000 in addition to its original price. We installed a venting and drainage system on the roof. A crepe machine, a robot kitchen, raclette machines, external painting, menus, and storage boxes were added.

Renting or buying a Food Truck

You can sometimes rent a food truck as an alternative to buying it. It's not very popular and has not been seen in use, but it might be worth looking into if you are interested in trying out the concept before investing your money. We were fortunate to be able to meet some of the owners, who were selling their trucks. In the meantime, we are renting it out. Don't hesitate to reach out to the seller if there are no ads for food trucks available for sale. You might face some problems when renting a truck. You may find it annoying to have to refuse to host events because the food truck isn't available. You are able to be more flexible, and you can order your food truck whenever you want. We needed to eat our food truck, as we had an idea in mind. We considered renting the food truck, but ultimately decided to sell it. It took us many months before we found a serious buyer. We eventually decided to abandon the idea due to the complexity of administrative procedures required (since the trailer and insurance were registered under our names). The decoration had been painted on the food trailer. It would have also been difficult for others if they tried to modify it to fit their needs.

Building a brand new vehicle

A modified truck can be constructed if there isn't a truck available with the configuration you require. It is better to have the truck setup exactly as you wish, than having to deal a truck with an inadequate kitchen. The downside to getting your vehicle is that this is often the most expensive option and can take a long time before it is ready for you.

Most trucks built on demand can take anywhere from five to seven working weeks before being delivered to their destination. You need to make sure the truck gets delivered on time. You will look very unprofessional if your truck is late to your opening day of your new food company.

If you intend to build your own truck, be sure to find a local truck building company that is familiar with local health code regulations. A professional designer will assist in the speeding up of the construction process and review the work according to the health department inspection.

You can purchase a used car

The best condition a truck can be purchased is the one you have to pay for. You may end up paying thousands for repairs or purchasing a 20 year-old truck. It will also cost you sales. You don't make money on the lane every day your vehicle sits in the shop because it is broken down. It might seem like a good idea to get started with a truck if you have a tight budget.

Consider the long-term, however. If you want to try any truck, make sure you have a reliable mechanic with you. It is important to ensure the costly items such as the engine, transmission and other parts are in excellent condition. Auctions are a great way to buy a used Phase Van. USPS and FedEx are the main users of phase vans in order to properly maintain their fleet vehicles. A professionally maintained fleet of step vans appears to be in better shape than one-owner ones.

Fuel

The cost of the gasoline or diesel in your locality can impact this decision. You should also consider engine life, mileage and availability. Diesel engines are generally more durable and require less maintenance. The engine's lifespan can be extended by 50 to 75 percent, according to some estimates. However, the maintenance depends on the engine. This engine is more difficult than a gasoline one and so it can be more costly to repair if the fuel distribution systems are not working properly.

Although gasoline offers greater acceleration, diesel engines deliver more torque. This makes them better suited to driving large trucks or buses. Because food trucks are slow but can stop quickly, diesel trucks provide more torque which translates into greater fuel efficiency. Diesel is 20 percent stronger, according to my mechanic. One drawback of diesel for people who have food trucks that are located in cold areas is the possibility of diesel sludge buildup in winter. From an ecological perspective, diesel is marginally more beneficial for the climate.

First, diesel engines can also be powered using biodiesel fuel. Biodiesel can be made using cooking oil. There is something poetic in lowering the cooking oils and then adding biodiesel. Made-up exhaust contains more particles than diesel fuel. These particles tend to fall quicker from the atmosphere and are less likely that they will be absorbed in the bloodstream.

Power

Food trucks need fuel in order to function. A generator is essential for any truck to be able to provide electricity for its basic requirements. But, if you are cooking, it is possible to choose how your generator will power your kitchen equipment. Propane or natural gas can be used for cooking. Propane is an inexpensive and easy-to-find fuel. It also has a high energy consumption. It is lightweight, environmentally-friendly, and very quiet. It can be used as a cooking gas, a power source, or to run cooling systems. Propanedol is strong.

There are not many moving parts so trucks rarely miss a day because of a propane system problem. Propane is a highly combustible gas that can prove to be a danger if it isn't handled properly.

Propane or natural gas may be required to cook meat or perform energy-intensive processes. However, it is worth considering leaving your propane tanks at home if they are not necessary. It's less reliable but it's easier and safer than using a diesel/gasoline generator to power your equipment. You only need one source of energy (if you run your generator from your fuel tank). Propane, if not handled properly, can prove to be extremely dangerous. If the propane isn't covered before driving it can cause a serious accident.

Electricity-powered trucks can be driven indoors, which is an exciting advantage. The indoor use of propane is typically not allowed due to the carbon monoxide produced by propane burning. This is something that many food trucks won't have, but if you have a large indoor venue, it may allow you to hold private events or provide indoor catering. If you plan on using propane, integrate the ability of running entirely off electricity. Perhaps it will be of use.

Decorate Your Truck

Your customers will decide whether you are a good business or not based on how your truck looks. I recommend working with a graphic artist to design a logo that represents the brand's core elements. They then help to implement the strategy with professionals. You can wrap, paint, or decorate your truck using vinyl stickers. Personally, I like painted vinyl stacker trucks. It's my preferred solution, as it is flexible, durable, and most cost-effective.

However, some operators may be reluctant to do this because corporate sponsors can sometimes purchase trucks and wrap them in advertising. Vinyl stickers can be damaged if the wrap is too thick. But it is not common for you to wrap up your truck in case. You would usually be asked by a sponsor to wrap up your truck again for the case.

Vehicle wrapping also goes by the names graphics for buses (transit graphics), transit advertising, transit graphics, transit advertising and decals. Wraps are an efficient and fast way to get your truck branded. A vinyl film is used to wrap your truck. It can be printed by a truck wrapping firm or general printing company and then applied. Cast vinyl and calendar Vinyl are also available.

Naming your Truck

The name of your food truck might not make or break it, but having the right proper title can make a big difference to your success, especially in the early stages. It is important to start branding your mobile company with a memorable name. This is the first step towards creating a strong brand. Your food truck name should be memorable. It should make people feel something.

The name you choose will be the first impression people have about your mobile company. If you're new to the area, and people don't have much information about you or your business, their first impression of you will be your chosen name.

To test an idea, you can let your family or friends know the name and ask them what picture they think of. What would your family expect if they heard this name as they approached your vehicle? Ask them for details about everything. The more information you can give, the better your understanding of the name's effectiveness.

Do this with many names. Get rid of any that don't work.

HOW TO STAND ON A RIGHTED WAY OF LAW

A

As a food truck owner, you will be subject to many laws. There are many rules that can be restrictive and so you might feel like giving up. You won't feel discouraged. Laws and regulations are difficult to understand at first but you will eventually grasp it. You shouldn't attempt to get them all in one go.

There are two main regulations you need to adhere to: federal and state. Federal laws don't need much and are relatively light. As long as you do not serve alcohol or tobacco, federal laws don't apply to your business. State laws are more pertinent to your business and can be more complex. Local regulations are often the most stressful. This can make it difficult to research. It is important to spend the time researching local laws before you can start your business. It is best to do this research before writing a business planning. You will find it easier to follow these rules after you've learned them.

Licenses and regulations fall into four categories: parking laws and requirements, local licensing requirements and commissary needs, and the standards of the health code. This will require a lot of time and bureaucracy. You can expect some frustrations along this path.

It is best to start with federal laws, as they are the least needed. All you need is to form a business or get an Employee Identification number (EIN). You have three options when it comes to business structure: corporation, partnership, or sole proprietorship. After you have settled on a business model, you need to file for an EIN. This will allow you to file your tax. If you aren't hiring employees, you may file taxes using your social safety number (SSN). Next, you can apply for an EIN by yourself or have your accountant do it for you. After you have received your EIN number, you can open an Account. Your EIN is activated after 30 days.

All aspects of the food-truck industry are governed by law. You may be subject to several laws depending on where your business is located. Make sure you do thorough research about the laws applicable to your region.

* Employment laws: These are laws governing the hiring and dismissal of employees. It also covers employee rights and safety.

* Tax laws refer to tax returns and payments. It covers corporate taxes, state taxes and other tax-related matters.

* Business formation laws: These are laws to apply to different business structures

* These laws apply to consumers and are intended to protect them from unfair or fraudulent business practices.

* Trademark and Patent Laws - These are laws about intellectual property and ownership.

* Environmental laws also include disposal of hazardous materials your truck or commercial food preparation may produce, and recycling regulations.

* Zoning Laws include local permits and licenses as well signage.

While you might be excited about your food truck business, you can also be busy with the creative aspect of the venture without worrying about the legalities. Although it might seem counterintuitive to consider the added cost that a lawyer and an accountant may cause, it is still a good idea to use them. Do not try to do it all yourself. You can also benefit from their expertise and knowledge of the area.

How to handle the Law's challenges

Understanding the law can be very difficult and feel like you are heading for a struggle. It's important to arrange for everything in order not to lose sight of the goal. Here are some tips to deal with these situations:

Be ready to comply with restrictive laws

Many believe the best thing about a food truck is its ability move around and park where you wish and to start serving food right away. That is not true. There are strict regulations regarding where a food cart can park and how it can sell its product. Boston, for example, has a law prohibiting food trucks from parking within a specified distance from a restaurant. Additionally, they cannot remain in the same area for more than a few hours each day. There are laws that prohibit food trucks operating in certain areas. These are some restrictions that you might encounter. But don't assume everything will be fine.

Some places limit the size of your truck and restrict what you are allowed to serve. Other places require you not to take food outside of a specified area. These laws can be complicated so it is worth spending at least one calendar month researching your local laws. While I understand that learning about these laws can be difficult, you need to be committed to your success.

Assume That There are No Laws

Some cities don't have the laws yet to allow food trucks. It is important that you are prepared to explain what your business does and how it operates. In these cases, it would be helpful to keep calm. It is important to assume restaurant laws, especially if you live in an area that does not have any laws regarding food trucks. You should be aware that the government can change existing laws.

Gather Information

Survival requires all your weapons. Information is the most powerful weapon you can have. Before you can identify the problem, gather and classify your data. You have now identified the need to find information. The next step is to get that information.

Information is available from many sources. The most common being the Internet. Information is available online. We have many food truck websites which are rich in information. These sites offer endless resources for your food truck business. You can also subscribe the google news bulletin to be informed about the most recent changes in the sector. There is always a risk of getting false information from the internet. Make sure to research reliable and trusted sites.

The local government offices can be a great resource of information. This section contains information on the laws, including the local chambers or commerce, the health department, small business administration, and other relevant departments. All information about food trucks can be found on their website. If not, it is worth visiting their local office.

Food truck associations are another good source of information. They can be a great helper and have the experience to guide you.

A lot of food truck owners join forces to form an organization. These associations collect information about what you need to get started as well as answer common questions that food truck owners have when starting a business. Another benefit is the networking. You can get more information from the group and receive life-saving tips. If you are unsure if such an organisation exists in your locality, ask the owner of a food truck. You can also search online for more information.

To avoid any misinterpretation, it is essential to classify information. You will need information about truck specifications, licenses. Information about where you can store your stuff, safety, health, and how to apply for your licence. Information about insurance. One example of this information is: what type do you need? What are the requirements for zoning? Which area can I park in? What are the requirements for food trucks? Safety and health regulations? What type insurance do you require?

These questions all require answers that will aid you in your business. If you are able to answer at least one of these questions then you will be more secure.

Organize Yourself

Organization is a wonderful skill. But, with the volume and complexity of the information you will be gathering you will need to learn it. Information overload can easily occur with this amount of information. You could also lose valuable information. The organization is easy to understand. The rule of thumb is to take each piece one by one. Here are some tips to improve your organizational skill.

* Create a checklist. This is the best way you can track everything and gather all of the information that you need. You'll be able to tell the difference between things you've done and those that are still being worked on. You will be able to distinguish what you have worked on and those that have not been touched.

* Store: Keep all information in one place. Take scanned documents and save them in a folder. It acts as a backup in case the original folder is lost.

* Keep records. Keep a log of all conversations, contact information, and other details.

* Schedule time. Make sure you have enough time to collect your information. It doesn't really matter if it takes you three days a week, or a single hour per day. What matters is that you create a schedule. And then stick to it. Be aware that many people you will be speaking with are busy and would prefer an appointment. It helps keep things organized.

* Consistency when dealing with officials. Fill out all forms the same way and pitch your business. This will reduce the chance of being confused.

LICENSES & PERMITS for YOUR FOOD TRUCKING COMPANY

Rules and Regulations

T

This section focuses on the legal requirements to be aware of before you open a food truck. Many of the rules that regulate the industry are different in each city. To avoid legal issues, it's important to read these carefully. This article will discuss a few rules that can be used to guide food trucks businesses.

Establishing the Structure of Your Company

Before you begin to build the structure for your food truck, it's important to know whether you'll be operating the business alone or with other owners. The latter is called a partnership. If you want to protect your assets against losses, you can make your business a corporation. This is what we refer to as a "limited liability business".

Limiting your liability can help reduce the business losses it sustains. This makes it almost seem like your company is an entity independent of you, and is responsible for all its losses. If the business is in debt or issued, it would not affect your assets. Talk to a lawyer about how to get your company incorporated.

Incorporating business can bring with it additional costs and requirements.

* Filing fees

* Publication fees

* Franchise taxes

* All legal fees

* Corporate recordkeeping, etc.

The above mentioned factors could make it more difficult to set up your company. As such, it is recommended to wait until a later time before incorporating it. It is possible to register your business as a sole proprietorship. After that, you can apply for a business certificate. These certificates are available at a minimal cost. All the remaining steps can be done online.

Get your EIN

Employer Identification Number. It's not easy to manage a food-truck business. You have to organize the kitchen and take care of the customers. This is why you need people to assist you.

An EIN is required for all employees. After that, each employee should be issued an I-9 form and then they must complete a W-4. Also, you will need to pay the employer's social security and Medicare taxes. For federal and state income taxes to be paid, you will need a percentage of the employees' earnings. Last but not least, you'll need to pay for worker's insurance.

Get the Licenses and Permits You Need

It is essential to obtain the required permits and licenses when you plan to start a food truck operation. It is easy to fall prey to the law by failing to address this issue. You could end up spending all of your profits on fines and having to close your business. Here are some licenses that you need to obtain for your business.

Food Service Business License

Before you are allowed to start a food-truck business, you need this license. This license will be issued by the municipality in which you intend to run your business. Some municipalities require you to renew the company every year. It may only be once every two years. It is important to renew your license every year in order to avoid your license being expired.

To obtain a food service license, you will need to state the purpose of your company's existence. You could supply food delivery services or other services related to food. You need to be as precise as possible in order to have your license approved.

License for Food Handlers

This license is issued in the location where your food cart will be. It allows you to provide food services to residents. This license is subject to different requirements. You might have to be examined in some cases. You can enroll in several training courses that will help you prepare for this exam.

Permits for Safety and Health

Food truck owners should realize that getting all the licenses is not enough. These licenses must be renewed each year. You would need to renew them as often as possible because health officials will usually map out regular inspections on the truck in order to ensure that it meets all food safety requirements. Another thing to watch out for is that your business may be closed if these conditions are not met.

The following are the items that food truck drivers must be inspected by health inspectors:

* The storage of food. You need to make sure that food is stored in the right temperature and under the right conditions.

* If the food is being handled by people wearing gloves.

* Cleanliness of equipment used in cooking.

* If your food truck meets all health and fire codes.

Permits for Electricity and Gas

Food trucks are essential to cooking. Gas or electricity are required to start a fire. It is important that your cooking equipment is free of hazards and dangers. Make sure to check your equipment on a regular basis to ensure safety. You don't want to be in a position where someone finds fault with any equipment.

Commercial Vehicle License

A license is required for every food truck that you operate. Vehicles usually get licenses based on their weight, length, and height.

Driver's Licence

First, identify who will be driving your food truck. If you're hiring someone to drive your food truck, make sure they have a driver's license. If you're driving the truck yourself, it is also important. The driver's permit is required to allow you to drive a food cart on public roads. Make sure you check when your license expires to make sure that you renew it as soon and as quickly as possible.

Get your Food Truck Certified

Insurance is required in several states for food trucks to be insured. You might need to have commercial auto insurance if you own a truck. General liability insurance is necessary if you intend to take your food truck into areas that are crowded. Workers insurance must be purchased when you employ workers to your business.

There are several types of insurance that you might need. These depend on your services and your business. So that you are able to choose the right insurance for your truck, let's take a look at some of the options.

* Commercial Vehicle Insurance: This type helps cover damage from vehicle accidents.

* Property insurance: This policy covers your truck, cooking equipment, and other property in case of theft.

* General Liability: This policy covers damage that is not directly related your vehicle.

* Workers' Compensation: This insurance can be used by most states to pay for workers' compensation costs resulting from accidents at work.

* General insurance: While the price of general auto insurance varies by state, it typically runs at around $2400 annually.

It is also important to know what factors can influence the amount of money that you spend on insurance.

* Your coverage limits

* The type of food truck you use to run your business

* State and city in which your food truck is located

* The total value of your personal property

* The events and locations that you attend each year

* The operation's time limit

* Seasonality in your food truck company

* The equipment that you can move and the equipment that is permanently installed.

* Parking Restrictions, Zoning

Many cities and towns have zone restrictions today that prohibit you from simply parking your truck anywhere. These restrictions may be used to restrict movement of food trailers and food trucks to restricted areas. The county clerk can help you find these places. The two-hour parking limit may also apply to you.

When parking your truck, ensure you are not too far from the curb. You should also ensure that your truck does not double-park. To learn more, you can contact your local vehicle department.

Before you Launch, Learn About Local Regulations and Rules

Food trucks are similarly regulated as the restaurant industry. The regulations cover truck construction and sales. Because they affect all aspects of your business, it is essential to understand and comply with the local regulations. There are many laws that will govern everything about your food truck. From what food you may serve to where your vehicle can be parked to whether you have the right to sell your food to customers, all of them will apply. It would be difficult to list all of the laws applicable to food trucks. This book is too large. Here are a few. Get to know the laws that are most likely to impact your business (or hire someone who does).

Before buying the stepvan that you've been keeping track of on eBay TM, it is important to review all local laws and regulations relating the food truck sale in your community. Local regulations play an important part in the decision making process for several aspects of your business. How your truck can make it, how it will operate, and who your staff will be will all be affected by local regulations. To ensure compliance with local laws and regulations, any potential food truck entrepreneur must first study them.

Local laws are best studied in depth. Ask for clarifications from other suppliers or go online to read descriptions. You need to dig deeper into the regulations in order to fully understand them. You can find out the details of the local laws by visiting your local health office. If you have any questions, contact the local health department.

Also, make sure to visit the person in charge of mobile foods at your health department. When you face potential regulatory issues or questions, it is helpful to have a partner in these departments with a decision maker.

An entrepreneur operating in mobile food services must be familiar and able to understand local regulations. They can be laminated so you have them at all times until you get them mastered.

Licenses

A license, which is a legal document granted by a government body, allows you to do any or all of the things that are permitted. In certain cases, licensing may be issued after an inspection. However, a business licence is usually not subject to any review.

Food trucks are restricted in one way: they can serve any type of food. A common distinction is between trucks that prepare food from the truck, such burgers, tacos, or waffles. Non-processing trucks sell pre-packaged and off-site prepared food. The key difference between production trucks and non-processing trucks is the fact that they present a greater risk for public health because they prepare food containing food-borne diseases. Modern processing methods make it possible for trucks to safely sell processed food. Over time, local laws might catch up to the realities.

Vehicle License

First, you need a vehicle registration in order to move your truck on the roads. You will need a vehicle license to drive your truck. The driver behind the wheel should also have a driving permit. Depending on the size and weight of the truck, some states require that a commercial driver's licence be obtained in order to operate it.

Business License

You will need a business permit to begin selling your items once your truck is out on the street. A business licence is your company's legal identity that allows you work in your specific market. The Constitution requires small companies to get the required business license from the federal or local government before they deliver goods or services. This license is necessary to register your business with government in order for you to pay taxes on your gross profits.

License Tax

This number is your social insurance number. You will also need an EIN, employer identification number, if the business you run is sole proprietorship. In some states, you may need sales or franchise licenses to ensure compliance.

State Permits

A permit can be described as a license issued by government entities. Permits, which are typically issued for protection purposes, are typically granted after an examination. The permits you need to start your company may vary depending on the state. For more information, visit the SBA Licenses and Permits website.

Local Permits

Other permit requirements may apply to your municipality for things like signs, zoning taxation or alarms. For more details, please refer to the above links and the official city website.

Some street markets offer street vending on public streets. The available hours and places often restrict street vending. Usually, trucks must sell the same products at a fixed distance to other businesses. Street vending allows you to access more sales locations but is difficult because there is always competition. Some municipalities only allow food carts or food trucks on private lots. Lot sales are very popular in markets like Austin, Portland, and Los Angeles. Lots are also a very popular option in markets where street selling is allowed, such as Los Angeles or New York City.

Food license

Just like a restaurant needs to be inspected by the health department, your mobile restaurant will need approval from the local department of health to ensure that food is properly preserved.

Liquor License

A liquor license would be required to allow you to sell alcohol with your food truck. This license isn't easy to obtain because it depends on where you intend to operate your business.

Music License

A music license will be required in order to play copiedrighted content to your customers. This will depend on where your business operates. You may need to obtain a license if your music is from other CDs.

Requirements for Employers

Before you can hire legal staff, you need to make sure that they are legally allowed to work in your area. Employers in the United States have to submit I-9s that prove job eligibility and W-4s which assess income tax mitholding. The IRS provides additional information on the tax guide for employers. Employers might have to place such posters on their premises. For more information about employee benefits, unemployment coverage, or auto/general liability coverage, please contact an experienced insurance professional.

Keep Other Liabilities in Mind

When you are sole proprietor, your personal responsibility will be for work-related incidents, food poisoning, and any collisions. As such, it is recommended that you consult a lawyer about the possibility to create a company (or LLC) which will protect your personal assets against business publicity. Many states offer training forms that can be downloaded free of charge on their Secretary Of State Websites.

You cannot manage all the permits and licenses required for mobile food vendors because they are linked to different government departments. It can be difficult to acquire all necessary paperwork. There will likely be multiple follow up calls so be prepared to wait.

To find out the time it took for the license process to be completed, speak to other owners. Expect to have to submit to inspections.

After all these laws and regulations, food trucks still work well in cities. They get customers out on the road and help build community. Food trucks activate public spaces and generate tax revenues for local governments. Many economists believe small businesses are the main driver for job growth. Food trucks operate independently and are a part of local communities that contribute to the development of their customers. They buy local products, hire local employees, and sell directly to local clients.

www.ingramcontent.com/pod-product-compliance
Lightning Source LLC
Chambersburg PA
CBHW050403120526
44590CB00015B/1805